# WIN AT HEARTS

## Joseph D. Andrews

Bonus Books, Inc., Chicago

02  01  00  99  98                                    5  4  3  2  1

Library of Congress Catalog Card Number: 98-72846

International Standard Book Number: 1-56625-110-9

**Bonus Books, Inc.**
160 East Illinois Street
Chicago, Illinois 60611

Playing cards on cover courtesy of The United States Playing Card Company

Printed in the United States of America

*This book is dedicated
to my daughter,
Laurie Elizabeth,
"The Queen of Hearts"*

# PREFACE

Hearts has been called one of the most vicious "cutthroat" card games ever created. It arrived on the scene more than one hundred years ago, and remains an American favorite. This game is usually an individual's contest, with each player trying to outwit and "psych" his opponents!

Hearts, is a very easy game to learn. However, there is no substitute for experience! This game provides a perfect setting for the application of skill in interpreting the meaning of your opponents' plays, and in the planning of your own strategy. Part of the fascination of Hearts is its *reverse* scoring, with the emphasis on gathering as *few* points as possible. Another curiosity is the Slam (known as "shooting the moon"), which rewards the successful player who manages to capture all of the points in the same deal! Of course, there is the ultimate weapon—the dreaded Queen of Spades. This is the card that strikes fear in your opponents, and creates a lot of excitement!

The increased popularity of the Internet, as well as many fine Hearts CD programs have helped to re-kindle interest and introduce more people to this classic game. This book illustrates basic, intermediate, and advanced strategy. You will learn excellent technique from many expert contributors. There are plenty of illustrative hands which will help you to improve your game. Someday, you may have the opportunity to compete for a national championship or test your skills against the "pros" on the Internet!

Good luck, and good Hearts!

—JOSEPH D. ANDREWS, 1998

# FOREWORD

BY RANDY WHEELER

By legend, Hearts began with all 52 plane★ people of the world divided equally into four classes: warriors, clergy, merchants, and peasants, all ruled by four gods. These gods shuffled all the people at random and distributed them to the four corners of the globe, North, East, South, and West. The gods held a contest for all things of value that each held dear. And each god, by law, selected three people, whom he then banished from the common weal of his realm; then each god accepted the undesirables from the other realms with the hope of improving the lot of all in his own kingdom.

By agreement, that god having in his realm the world's poorest peasant sent him forth to reconnoiter, and each god in his turn sent forth a peasant, if possible, to join the lowliest. Twice more peasants sallied and assembled in foursomes, in so doing revealing the strength of other positions.

Cautiously, the North god, smiled upon by the mistress of war, unfolded the mighty power of his church and clergy and collected unto himself all the Holy Grails from the four corners of the plane world. Furthermore, nothing could stop the juggernaut, as all things held dear fell into possession of the mighty North god. This included Pallas (the evil lady).

After much discussion of what might have been, the gods again shuffled and randomly distributed all plane people four ways over the earth. And it came to pass that a desire for these things held so dear to all brought reason for the people again to be called forth to battle, and, once again, all things held dear were contested for, though rarely monopolized. And again the contest was repeated, and yet again—ad infinitum.

★Geometrically, every playing card is a plane. (J. D. A.)

# CONTENTS

Chapter One    HEARTS: A BRIEF HISTORY
        by George S. Coffin                                 1

Chapter Two    A BRIEF OVERVIEW         5
        The Players        5
        The Pack        5
        The Pass        6
        The Opening Lead        6
        The Object of the Game        7
        Scoring        7
        Heart Lead Prohibited        8

Chapter Three  THE PASS AND OTHER BASICS        9
        The Pass        9
        Insurance Against the Slam        11
        Defensive Discards        13
        Illustrative Hand        14

Chapter Four   SPADE-SUIT MANAGEMENT        16
        Basic Situations        16
            The Spear Play        16
            The Double Spear        17
            Hold-up Play        18
            The Collins Gambit        20
            Passes to the Right        21
        More on Spades        22
            The Rubin Maneuver        23
            The Rosner Suicide Pass        23
            Holding of Poorly Guarded Ace or King        24
            The Scatter Pass Technique        25
            The Overloaded-Queen Syndrome        26

| | | |
|---|---|---:|
| Chapter Five | PLANNING YOUR PLAY | 27 |
| | Planning and Strategy | 27 |
| | Control Cards (Exit Cards) | 29 |
| | Ducking | 30 |
| | Remembering Spot Cards | 30 |
| | The Orin Johnson Maneuver | 30 |
| | The Value of Slam | 31 |
| | The Slam ("Moonshot," "Smudge") | 32 |
| | | |
| Chapter Six | DEFENSIVE PLAY | 34 |
| | Foresight | 34 |
| | Defense Under Pressure (The Pseudo-Squeeze) | 36 |
| | The Strip Play ("Grand Exit") | 37 |
| | Strip Technique: The Backward Strip | 39 |
| |   The Wrong Way | 39 |
| |   The Right Way | 40 |
| |   Strip Play—Advanced | 41 |
| | "With a Little Bit of Luck": The Evans Moon | 42 |
| | The Endplay | 43 |
| | Endgame Positions | 45 |
| | | |
| Chapter Seven | PSYCHOLOGY IN HEARTS | 47 |
| | The Hog | 48 |
| | Fear of Slam | 50 |
| | The Phony Smoke | 51 |
| | The False Card | 52 |
| | The Slow Torture | 54 |
| | The Technician | 56 |
| | The Shaft (I) | 57 |
| | The Shaft (II) | 59 |
| | The Soderlund Squeeze—Variety I | 61 |
| | | |
| Chapter Eight | HEARTS VARIATIONS | 63 |
| | Partnership Hearts, or Doubles | 63 |
| |   Introduction | 63 |
| |   The High-Low, or Echo | 65 |
| |   Unblocking | 67 |
| |   Communication by Inference; | |
| |     Cooperation; Clearance | 68 |
| |   The Vienna Coup | 71 |

Partnership Hearts—Variety II Strategy and
Technique 74
Jack of Diamonds (Plus Ten) 76
Jack Becomes Master 77
Dropping the Jack 77
Diamond Jack Led Up To 77
Void in Diamonds; Jack-of-Diamonds Endplay 79
Trio Hearts: A Challenge for Three 81
Basic Trio 81
Slams in Trio 81
Spade Guards for the Queen 81
Count and Strip 82
Two-Handed Hearts 83
Background and Rules 83
Strategy 85
Depravation Play—Part II85 85

Chapter Nine FINAL HAND: THE GRAND SQUASH 88

Chapter Ten "A DAY IN THE LIFE" (DIARY OF
A HEARTS PLAYER) 91

Appendix One "UNCLE" JOE'S TEN WINNING
HEARTS TIPS 99

Appendix Two GLOSSARY OF TERMS 101

Appendix Three THE LAWS OF HEARTS 111

Appendix Four DUPLICATE HEARTS 121

Appendix Five THE INTERNET 123
THE AMERICAN HEARTS AND SPADES
PLAYERS' ASSOCIATION 125

# Chapter One
# HEARTS: A BRIEF HISTORY
BY George S. Coffin

Hearts evolved from a game played around 1750 in Spain, called "reversé." In that game the ♡J was called "quinola grande" (great quinola) and the ♡Q was the "little quinola" or "espagnolette." Each of these cards scored many black (i.e., negative) points against their captors. In similar games also called "reversé," or "reversis," the usual object of play was to *lose* tricks, not to win them. In another ancestor of Hearts, the game of four jacks, the object was to avoid winning in a trick any Jack, which scored one black point, or 2 points in the case of the ♠J. In other variants other cards were the skunks (i.e., scored negative points).

Around 1850, reversis gave way to simple Hearts. According to Albert H. Morehead and Geoffrey Mott-Smith in *Culbertson's Hoyle* (New York, 1950), the game of Hearts was "simple as to rules, but difficult as whist to play well. This austere game has been greatly popularized during the past fifty years by the addition of certain features that add to the variety and also tend to make the game easier to play at."

The game of Hearts in a sense favors players with *losing* hands. To win you need plenty of what in other games would be losing cards, such as deuces and treys, in order to avoid capturing negative (black-point) cards, and the entire heart suit, which consistent losers presumably hold in such "positive" games as whist and bridge. Even in the latter two games, optional forms came to be introduced to encourage

1

consistent holders of "bad" cards. The simplest of these forms was "nullos," where the aim was to lose tricks. The poor-card holders, however, soon complained that in nullos they became loaded with Aces, Kings, and Queens.

Later, an ingenious Yankee invented a neat solution to this problem, "reversi bridge." The holder of bad cards could *reverse* the rank of every card and convert a deuce into an Ace, a trey into a King, a four into a Queen, etc., simply by adding the word "reversi" to his bid. To cater to his ilk a special boxed game of 52 reversible, domino-like cards was issued in 1938 by Bridge Headquarters of New York City. Each card tile was printed with one rank on the top half and its reversi counterpart on the bottom, such as ◇A on the top end and ◇2 on the bottom. The reversi halves of all card tiles were printed in a different color. The player simply moved a metal slide up or down in order to expose only the desired halves of the 13 card tiles of his bridge hand to make them regular or reversi. In later years a regular pack of reversible cards made a brief appearance in the bridge market. With these, you simply turned a ♣2 upside down to convert it into the ♣A.

These devices to please poor-card holders, which like the earlier nullos were designed to lose tricks in auction bridge, were never officially recognized, so nullos and reversi vanished quickly from the bridge scene.

The real aim of the game of Hearts, however, is not to placate poor-card holders. It is not a game that simply features top and bottom cards, like bridge and reversi. It also elevates intermediate cards to key importance. These are Jacks down through sixes, which possess little control power, but which form a dumping ground of bad luck to draw black-point cards to the tricks of their unfortunate holders.

Various embellishments over the centuries have enlivened the basic forms of many card games, and a few of genuine merit have persisted permanently. And so the variation of yesterday becomes the standard of today, and today's new variation may become the standard of tomorrow. In the olden whist days of our grandfathers, some chap disliked having to turn his last card as dealer to determine trump, only to find it a singleton in his hand with seven cards of another beautiful suit, maybe A K Q J x x x. To avoid such maddening quirks of chance, the bright chap introduced dealer's right to name his best suit for trump. Later another player conceived of the idea of "passing the buck" with a 4-3-3-3 shape by the dealer's *bridging* to his partner this right to

name trump. A few years later one of three whist players stuck without a fourth proposed the exposed dummy hand. Next came bid whist,
a competitive auction in numbers of odd tricks only; here, only after
the auction was closed was the trump suit named, by the highest bid
der of course. And someone introduced no-trump bidding and play
that scored double or nearly so.

Around the turn of the century came the most startling innovation,
"auction bidding." A trump suit (or no-trump) was proposed as a part
of each bid, which had to outrank the previous bid in score value or
number of tricks and/or suit rank. Finally in 1925, in Paris, the late
Harold S. Vanderbilt, multimillionaire yachtsman, learned the French
game of "plafond" (literally, "ceiling") in which you score only your
"ceiling," or number of tricks that you bid to win toward game. Based
on this, in the same year Vanderbilt "invented" "contract bridge," in
which you could not score game unless you had bid it. To this, Vanderbilt added special huge premiums for slams *bid* and made. Soon Ely
Culbertson added the last major element, "vulnerability," which simply offset the advantage of those partners who had already won a game
toward rubber, by making them suffer greatly increased penalties for a
defeated contract.

Poker, even good poker for high stakes, had a development similar to
that of bridge. Originally, only cards linked by rank made up a hand,
such as two sevens, two pairs, three of a kind, etc.; flushes and
straights, introduced around 1860, were at first regarded in the South
as "the acme of vulgarity." Despite this, flushes and runs did become
standard. In parlor and family games, bets were limited to minuscule
amounts. Such limits deprived poker of the element of bluff, because
you simply cannot run a man out of a pot with a ten-cent bet. Home-
parlor poker limited to draw and five-card stud became dull, so, to re-
store excitement, players blessed with Yankee inventive genius
introduced a legion of novelties, such as "deuces wild," "spit-in-the-
ocean," "Southern Cross," and Lord only knows what else.

Like poker, the game of Hearts lends itself to the addition of almost
endless novelty variations. But unlike those in poker, such additions
were not meant to induce the equivalent of high-stake gambling fever,
but were improvements in the potential gamesmanship of the play. In
the original simple game, each heart that you won on a trick counted
one black point against you—period. If you took all thirteen hearts,
you got thirteen black points. As time passed, various embellishments

were added, finally raising the game to the level of tournament quality.

In the first of these changes, if a player collected all thirteen hearts, he won a slam worth thirteen white, or good, points, which he subtracted from his total of bad, or black, points. Next came Her Highness, "the black widow," ♠Q, scoring thirteen black points, but these changed to twenty-six white points if won with all thirteen hearts. To promote more action, each player usually passed three cards to an opponent. Finally, two good refinements appeared and, like the above, became standard. One was that no one could lead a heart unless a heart had been discarded or the ♠Q played on a previous trick. The other rule was the mandatory ♣2 opening lead, with the discard of a point card forbidden, if avoidable, on trick one. Also, with three, five, six, and seven players, the entire pack came to be dealt out as far as it would go, those players with extra cards playing *two* cards, clubs if possible, on trick one, to equalize their number of cards in hand for later tricks.

# Chapter Two
# A BRIEF OVERVIEW

The basic rules and principles of Hearts are simple.

## THE PLAYERS

The best game is four-handed, the usual party and tourney game, yet there are good variations for two to seven players. Three-handed is excellent. We will consider the four-handed game as the standard. The term "Cutthroat" applies to the variation of Hearts where each participant plays "solo" (individually). There is also a partnership variation, which is very challenging.

## THE PACK

A standard fifty-two card pack is used. The cards of each suit rank Ace high, King, Queen, Jack, ten, on down to the deuce. There is no trump, and all suits are equal. Cards are dealt face down one at a time until the pack runs out, as in bridge or whist.

## THE PASS

After the deal is completed, players should sort their cards in a logical fashion. It is best to separate the suits by color and arrange the cards from highest to the lowest-ranked within each suit. This allows for easy identification of all cards in the hand. Each player evaluates his hand (see the section, in the next chapter, on "The Pass"), removes any three cards that he does not want, and passes them *face down* to his LHO (left hand opponent).* Each player is not allowed to look at any passed cards until *after* he has passed his own three cards. Usually a player will pass high cards that threaten to capture point cards that count against him. On the second deal, the pass is made to the RHO (right hand opponent), and on the third to the OAT (opponent across the table). Then the rotation resumes with the pass to the LHO. In three-handed variations, the pass alternates from the LHO to the RHO, and so on. (For further details, see Law 6, "The Laws of Hearts," appendix 3.) The fourth deal of each hand may feature some additional passing options. One new variation is the "Scatter" Pass. Instead of passing three cards at one time, each player passes ONE card to each of his three opponents. Another relatively new option is the "keeper" or "hold" hand, where no cards are passed. Details regarding the Pass are reviewed in chapter 3.

## THE OPENING LEAD

After the pass is made, the player who holds the ♣2 must make the first play, called the opening lead. (The deuce-of-clubs lead has become the standard variation, replacing the original lead by the dealer or player on dealer's left.) He removes the ♣2 from his hand and places it face up on the center of the table. As in bridge and whist, the next player to his left likewise plays a card face up, then the third player, then the fourth. The player who played the highest card of the suit that led the trick wins the trick. He collects its four played cards together to form a neat packet, which he places face down in front of him. The winner of a trick leads to the next trick. One very trick a player must, if possible, play a card of the suit that led that trick, otherwise he must

*For definition of terms, see the Glossary (appendix 2).

*discard.* On this *first* trick only, no one is allowed to discard a heart or the ♠Q, unless unavoidable. Afterwards, the discard of the Queen of spades is *not* mandatory in order to play her, and she can be played at any (legal) opportunity after trick one. This enhances the positional play.

## THE OBJECT OF THE GAME

Every player aims to win the lowest score, as in golf. Thus, he tries to *avoid* capturing in tricks the *black-point* cards: the thirteen hearts, valued at one point each, and the ♠Q Pallas), valued at thirteen points. Or, rarely, he can try for *slam*, which consists of taking *all* fourteen point cards. When he accomplishes this, the cards' values are reversed, and he scores twenty-six *white* points. These points are not added but instead are *subtracted* from his regular black-point score to shrink it (*or*, if he chooses, twenty-six black points may be added to each opponent's score). White points are *good* to win. Tricks *per se* do not score. (The ♠Q is also called the black lady, the black widow, black Maria, etc., perhaps suggesting bad news, or, more specifically, the black-widow spider, who eats her mate.)

## SCORING

After the play of each deal ends, black points are counted and entered in each player's score column. In parties and tourneys most players move to other tables and meet new opponents. All play for simple cumulative scores. In one-table home games and in special tournaments the play is for "game," a prearranged total, such as 100 or 125 points. The first player to go game with the highest score is the *loser,* and the player with the lowest score is the *winner.* Tournament scores are match-pointed, with a player earning one match point for each player he defeated at his table. (A person may lay four or five games or "rounds" at the typical tournament.)

## HEART LEAD PROHIBITED

The last basic feature of the game is that no one may lead a heart until a heart has been discarded or the ♠Q has been played. But a player may lead the ♠Q anytime after trick one. If a player is reduced to the Queen of spades and all hearts (and no hearts have been played), that player announces that he has the spade Queen and hearts *only.* He now has the option of leading the Queen of spades or playing a heart of his choice. If a player holds nothing but hearts, and the Queen of spades has *not* been played, *and* a heart has not been played, this player must announce that he has all the hearts, and his lead of a heart (of his choice) is forced.

(For the finer points of the rules, be sure to read "The Laws of Hearts," appendix 3.)

# Chapter Three
# THE PASS AND OTHER BASICS

## THE PASS

An essential part of Hearts is the ability to make the proper pass. The correct technique will save you many points during the course of a typical game. Since you must face a passing decision at the beginning of every hand, it is in your best interest to learn this aspect of the game. The "scatter" pass and "hold" feature will be reviewed at the end of this chapter. For now, we will deal with the standard pass of three cards.

The chief feature of the pass is the opportunity it provides for you to improve your hand. Once you have diagnosed your holding, you ask yourself the question, "What shall I do?"

The first rule of passing is: **Analyze the spade suit.** Let's face it, spades is the key suit, and the Ace, King, and Queen are going concerns. If you are dealt the Ace *or* King with fewer than three other spades *lower* than the Queen (for example, A x x, K x x, A J, etc.),* you are *urged* to pass the Ace or King. These two cards are tailor-made for gobbling up the Queen, and you don't want either one in your hand with inadequate protection. An interesting gambit is the voiding of either minor (club or diamond suit) while retaining A x x or K x x of

*Each "x" signifies a "spot" card lower than the ten.

9

Spades. If you are passed no cards of your voided suit, you will be able to discard the high spade. The drawback to this technique is that you may be passed cards of the suit you voided, and then you will be in the same situation. Worse yet, you may "set up" your opponent for a chance to "Shoot the Moon"! If you are dealt the Queen of spades with only *three* other spades, you should consider keeping her if your other suits are very bad. Generally, the rule of thumb is to pass her with *fewer than four* spades of support. (See chapter 4, "Spade-Suit Management.")

The second rule of passing is: **Analyze the heart suit.** You have determined that your spade suit is safe or you have made the appropriate pass of the Ace, King, or Queen. Now it is time to review your hearts holding. Each high heart represents a potential of four points. Unless you hold the A K Q with great length (many cards in the suit), or A K Q J 10, etc., your high hearts may land you 8 or 12 points, and possibly the Queen of spades. Thus, you should make every effort to pass two and, possibly, all three of your bad hearts. This may allow an opponent to score slam, a far better result than eating 20 or 24 points all by yourself.

Of course, if your high hearts are accompanied by some nice low cards, such as the deuce, three, or four, you should consider passing your *second-highest* heart *only.* (It could stop a potential slam.) Never pass the singleton Ace. Avoid passing from such holdings as K x, Q x x, and J x x x. Each of these holdings represents a natural defense against slam.

The third and last rule of passing is: **Analyze your minor suits (clubs and diamonds).** As mentioned earlier, a suit with low cards is safer than one that has plenty of intermediates but no deuce, three, or four. After you have made your decision about your spade and heart suits, you must take stock of the minor suits. A suit with such cards as K J 10 8 7 is a strong candidate to fetch that nasty Queen. A suit with such cards as A K Q 10 8 5 3 2 is ironclad and almost immune from attack. Why is this so, especially since the latter suit is longer and contains more high cards? The answer is that they are *controls,* those nice low cards. The former suit is almost hopeless, as it includes (apart from great length) several cards above the seven. Every effort should be made to pass at least two, and, possibly, three cards from this holding. On the other hand, only an incredible lie of the cards could render the second holding useless. Don't waste time discarding from a suit like this. (I would, however, consider passing a short heart suit and setting up the potential of a slam.)

In summary, it is not the high cards in the minors that are dangerous—it is the *lack of low cards* that can be fatal. Also, a diamond or club holding with which you cannot duck a trick when you want to is a most inviting situation for a player who wants to blast you with the Queen of spades. Of course, all hands are different, and you must make a decision based on priorities.

## INSURANCE AGAINST THE SLAM

"Shooting The Moon" is the most devastating play in Hearts! It improves your position and score, and has a psychological effect on your opponents. The pass of a middle heart is the most effective defense against the Moon. Once your opponent knows you employ this defense, he will be reluctant to try for a Shoot. Then, on occasion, you can pass him three big diamonds or clubs. This has the effect of keeping him "off balance."

In Hearts, a main objective is to prevent enemy slams. This requires correct defensive passing and play. Suppose that you were dealt:

HAND A    ♠J 10 9 6    ♡Q 10 5 3    ◇A K    ♣K 6 4

It is tempting to pass the ◇A K and ♣K. But this could be dangerous, especially if the opponent receiving your pass holds either of the following:

HAND B    ♠A 8    ♡J 6    ◇Q 9 8 4 2    ♣A Q 9 7
HAND C    ♠A Q 5    ♡A 4    ◇Q 9 8    ♣A J 10 9 7

If Hand B passes his ♡J 6 and ♣8 (an obvious preparation for slam), your pass of the ◇A K and ♣K would send him on his way to triumph.

Hand C might pass the ♠Q 5 and the ♡4, and again a slam would be tried, thanks to your pass. Not every opponent to whom you pass is planning a slam, but why take the chance?

Suppose that with Hand A you passed the ♡10 and the ◇A K. You would control hearts with your Queen. Even if an opponent held hearts Ace-King eighth (♡ A K x x x x x x), he could not drop your Queen. She would stop him cold. Your only real problem is the ♣4;

but it would take a bad break in clubs to hurt you. Besides, your long spades are perfect to smoke out the Queen or to protect her if she was passed to you. Therefore, a good rule of thumb is to pass your *second-best heart* whenever possible, in order to prevent a slam by the receiver of your pass. Of course, another player at your table may be shooting for slam, but that is out of your control. And if you happen to be passing to a player dealt ♡A K Q J 10 x, etc., there is nothing you can do. Yet nine times out of ten the above technique is sound. There are some exceptions to the pass-hearts rule. For example:

HAND D     ♠4     ♡K 8 7 5 2     ◇Q 10 4     ♣K J 6 3

In this 1-5-3-4 shape spades are short. If you follow the rule and pass the eightspot of hearts and two clubs or diamonds, it might work well. But the danger is that your opponent might pass you the ♠A, ♠K, or ♠Q. Then your unguarded Queen might be dropped or your unguarded Ace or King might be led through (in this case, maneuvered into capturing an unwanted card). Here emergency measures must be taken. Try voiding yourself of diamonds, or of clubs if you have only three or fewer. Now if you are passed a tierce spade honor (A, K, or Q), you have a reasonable chance to park (i.e., discard) it. (Someone might lead a diamond before attacking spades.) Yes, your ♠Q could be smoked out, or you might be passed two diamonds and a high spade, but you can do nothing about these misfortunes. At least, trying to void yourself of clubs or diamonds gives you a *chance* to survive the worst. Remember too, that if an opponent knows that you pass him a heart every chance you get, he will assume that you will continue to do so. So he might not be so much inclined to try for slam. If you fail to pass him a low heart occasionally, your opponent will be thrown off balance, having expected you to pass him one as usual.

The time has come to review the newer passing options. The "scatter" pass has become quite popular in recent years, and is featured as an option on many of the Internet sites. Here, the strategy is a bit different. Remember, you are passing only one card to each of your opponents! If you have the high spade problem (A x x or K x x), the best "scatter" pass is the A or K to your immediate right, and a middle heart to each of your other opponents. (See chapter 4, "Spade Suit Management"). Another great "scatter" pass is one heart to each of your opponents or one middle or high minor suit card in the same fashion. A lot depends on the composition of your hand and priorities. Always think defensively!

Of course, "hold" or "keeper" hands present no passing problem; however, they must be played out, and particular attention must be paid to distributional percentages (refer to chapter 5, "Planning Your Play".) I personally do not support the "hold hand" option, as the pass is an inherent part of the game. I do know it has become quite popular and certainly is an acceptable option. Another interesting aspect of the "hold" hand is the fact that it is extremely difficult to "Shoot," and the luck factor tends to equalize or "level out" over the course of several games. There are many experts who demonstrate very fine technique while playing "hold" hands!

## DEFENSIVE DISCARDS

The outcome of many hands is decided by critical discards during the play. It would, therefore, be well for us to say a few words at this point about defensive discards. Suppose that after the pass you hold:

♠J 10 3    ♡K J 8 5 2    ◇A K 8    ♣Q 6

After two club leads, the ♣3 is led. The ♠Q has not appeared. Should you pitch a heart or a diamond? The hearts are fairly secure, but not the diamonds. The ◇8 may be vulnerable, especially on the third diamond lead. The ♠Q holder may have only two diamonds, which would make your eightspot a strong candidate to fetch the ♠Q. (The implications of situations like this will emerge more clearly later in this book.) If he has only one diamond, the second diamond lead could kill you. Why not improve your chances to avoid trouble? In this situation, it is advisable to discard your diamonds as soon as possible, and be rid of a potentially dangerous burden.

In general, if you hold a suit that has length or dangerous middle cards, and you have a chance to discard, try to pitch one of your troublesome high cards. If, however, you hold the length together with key *low* cards—3 2 or 4 3—you can afford to discard from another suit. It is usually good policy to avoid breaking (discarding) hearts early. This would give an opponent who might be in trouble a chance to escape in hearts, especially if he has an overloaded ♠Q. (See the next chapter, "Spade–Suit Management.")

## ILLUSTRATIVE HAND

A number of instructive and interesting hands are illustrated throughout this book. In order to help you follow each hand, a sample deal is shown below:

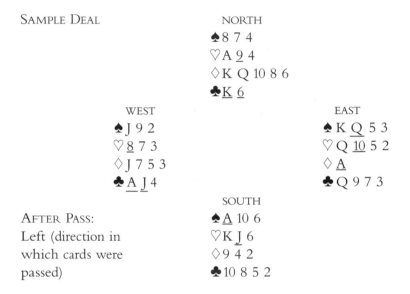

SAMPLE DEAL

NORTH
♠8 7 4
♡A 9 4
◇K Q 10 8 6
♣K 6

WEST
♠J 9 2
♡8 7 3
◇J 7 5 3
♣A J 4

EAST
♠K Q 5 3
♡Q 10 5 2
◇A
♣Q 9 7 3

SOUTH
♠A 10 6
♡K J 6
◇9 4 2
♣10 8 5 2

AFTER PASS:
Left (direction in
which cards were
passed)

Each player is designated by a compass direction. In most bridge columns, the North player is the hand shown nearest the top of the page. We will follow that format here. Each player's hand will indicate, by underlining, which cards the player received from his opponent. In this case, in the pass, South received the ♠A and the ♡J 6 (from East); West received the ♡8 and the ♣A J (from South), etc. The rotation of play is clockwise, the same as in whist or bridge.

South makes the required ♣2 lead; West plays the Ace, North drops the King, and East inserts the *seven,* a farsighted play. Next, West, leading, shifts to the ♠J, drawing the eight, five, and Ace. South continues with the ♠10, which is ducked by all. Then, with South still leading, on the following trick the ♠6 "rides around" to East's King. (Notice that it is not considered necessary to specify the play of every card. Remember that each player must contribute a card to each trick.) East is lucky; the suit has "broken" evenly, and his Queen is the thirteenth spade. The singleton ◇A is now cashed, followed by the ♣Q. South drops his ♣10, and West his ♣J. The ♣9 draws the ♣8, the ♣4, and the ♡9 discard from North.

Having partially completed the "strip," East ignores the hearts (the ♡2 allows him this luxury), and exits with the ♣3. South is in, his five fetches two high heart discards. He plays the ◇4, which is ducked by the three and taken by the Queen. East deposits the black lady on this trick. North escapes via the ♡4, which is covered by the five, and finally taken by South's King. The ◇2 throws North on lead (West is playing low), and he claims the balance.

Although the purpose of this deal is to familiarize you generally with the way a hand is played, the technique of the East player cannot escape notice. His careful club play on trick one allowed him to control and clear the suit at a later time (not to mention his clearance of the ◇A). The "strip" theme will be discussed in a later chapter. (See the section, "The Strip Play," in chapter 6.)

# Chapter Four
# SPADE-SUIT MANAGEMENT

## BASIC SITUATIONS

In Hearts, the spade suit is the most important. Familiarity with basic combinations and special techniques is essential if you want to become a skilled player. For example:

## The Spear Play*

DEAL 1
*The Spear Play*

NORTH
♠ K 7 6 5
♡ (Irrelevant)
♢ (Irrelevant)
♣ K 10 9

WEST
♠ J 10 9
♡ (Irrelevant)
♢ (Irrelevant)
♣ A 8

EAST
♠ 4 2
♡ (Irrelevant)
♢ (Irrelevant)
♣ J 7 6 5 2

SOUTH
♠ A Q 8 3
♡ (Irrelevant)
♢ (Irrelevant)
♣ Q 4 3

AFTER PASS:
Left

*Named by Bill Nicholls of Westford, MA

16

East has passed the ♠A Q to South. West wins the ♣2 opening and leads from ♠J 10 9. North has to duck every spade lead lest someone dump the Queen on his King, and South ducks twice. To trick four West leads his ♠9, North ducks, and East casts any card. South plays his Ace, capturing the lead. Then he pauses to count, thinking, "All followed suit twice, making eight spades. On the third round East discarded, 11 spades down. The King has not appeared, so 12 spades have been accounted for. My ♠Q is the thirteenth spade. So if I lead the Queen, she will spear the now dry King." ("Dry" indicates singleton or lone.)

## The Double Spear

Use of the spear play when available can save you from many a spade Queen. Simply count spades and keep track of the Ace and King. Perhaps once in a hundred deals the chance for a double spear occurs, too rare to worry about. Yet the principle is the same as for the standard spear play. We show this play as a curiosity. It actually occurred in a tournament (see Deal 2).

The pass was to left. West had been dealt a bad hand with the ♠A K. He elected to risk keeping the ♠K, and passed the ♡K J and ♠A. (This is best when dealt ♠A K x x.)★ Undoubtedly, West was hoping for a spade lead from North, expecting to play his King safely in last

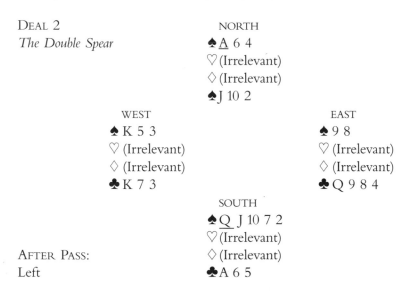

DEAL 2                                   NORTH
*The Double Spear*                       ♠A 6 4
                                         ♡ (Irrelevant)
                                         ◇ (Irrelevant)
                                         ♣J 10 2

              WEST                                          EAST
              ♠K 5 3                                        ♠9 8
              ♡ (Irrelevant)                                ♡ (Irrelevant)
              ◇ (Irrelevant)                                ◇ (Irrelevant)
              ♣K 7 3                                        ♣Q 9 8 4

                                         SOUTH
                                         ♠Q J 10 7 2
                                         ♡ (Irrelevant)
AFTER PASS:                              ◇ (Irrelevant)
Left                                     ♣A 6 5

★With ♠A K x x x, you should keep all of the suit; with ♠A K x, pass ♠A K.

position or perhaps discard it on another suit when led. South was dealt four spades and was not concerned when East passed him the ♠Q. But because South was winning and had many low cards in the minor suits, clubs and diamonds, he decided to be playful.

South won the ♣2 opening lead and switched to the ♠J! (See chapter 7, "Psychology in Hearts," for another example.) North and West, who did not know where the ♠Q was, both followed low. Next South led his ♠10; again North and West ducked. South stopped to count: eight spades played plus three spades left in his hand totalled 11. Neither Ace nor King had appeared; perhaps both were held by one player, perhaps they were divided. If these spade tops were massed (held by one player), the ♠Q lead must spear the Ace or King.

But a strange thing happened. East held neither Ace nor King, or else he would have played it safely in fourth position. South in a light-hearted vein (no pun intended) calmly led his ♠Q, his *spade Queen!* Then:

(1) South slowly pulled his hand away from the card he had played and concealed a wry grin.

(2) West rose with his King—he had no choice—and assumed he was dead.

(3) North was forced to cover with his now-dry Ace and groaned.

(4) East chortled and commented about the ♠A K Q all falling on one trick, as he discarded a high heart to fatten North's loss.

(5) South savored the occasion as he presented an instant replay on how well he had handled the spade suit.

(6) North glared, and the next hand was dealt quickly.

I suggest that when you make a spear play, maintain composure. Accept platitudes if they come, but, most important, *keep cool.* Don't rub salt into the wound of the speared player. Artistry is nice but a speared opponent might not appreciate it.

## Hold-up Play

Short holdings of four or fewer spades, including the Ace, King, or Queen, deserve study. For example, see Deal 3.

After the pass has been made and the first trick has been won by North, the latter leads his eightspot, East covers, South ducks, and west wins with his King. This removes the spear-play threat. West returns

DEAL 3
*Hold-up Play*

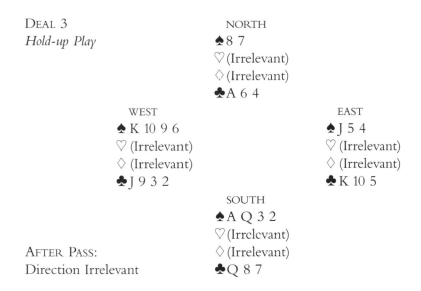

NORTH
♠ 8 7
♡ (Irrelevant)
◇ (Irrelevant)
♣ A 6 4

WEST
♠ K 10 9 6
♡ (Irrelevant)
◇ (Irrelevant)
♣ J 9 3 2

EAST
♠ J 5 4
♡ (Irrelevant)
◇ (Irrelevant)
♣ K 10 5

SOUTH
♠ A Q 3 2
♡ (Irrelevant)
◇ (Irrelevant)
♣ Q 8 7

AFTER PASS:
Direction Irrelevant

the ten, to which South responds with his Ace. South exits in another suit not shown and East *or* West wins; then *either* leads a spade—which smokes out the ♠Q. Some players in South would wail about the bad break, the lack of protection for the Queen.

Suppose that South holds up his ♠A until the *third* round (i.e., of spades), having let West's ten win the second. West having continued with the ♠9, South takes this trick with the ♠A. This leaves South with the ♠Q dry, and West still has the ♠6. But the difference is that North *and* East are now out of spades and cannot lead one to hurt South. Of course if West grabs the lead, South is dead, but it is better to have only *one* opponent who can hurt you instead of *two* or *three*.

If spades divide 4-3-3-3, South will survive regardless of normal play because his ♠Q will become a thirteener. But the 4-3-3-3 split is less likely to occur than the 4-4-3-2 or 4-4-4-1. Moral: hold up your high spade protection for as long as possible in order to exhaust an opponent or two of spades and reduce your chances later of a fatal spade lead.

The same principle applies if you hold the Ace or King without the Queen, and three low ones. If you get a lead up to your Ace-fourth hand, all is well. But if you hold ♠A 9 5 3 or ♠K J 7 4 or ♠A 9 5 2, play low on the first two leads. If an opponent persists in leading spades through you, you will be forced to play your second-best spade on the third round. If the Queen fails to drop, you will probably be speared;

if she does drop, you will have survived. By holding up your highest spade (besides the Ace or King), you stop spade leads temporarily, and you may be able to dump your top spade on the lead of another suit. The technique is similar in both cases (i.e., whether or not you hold the Queen). It will not guarantee your escaping the Queen, but it will at least improve your chances.

## The Collins Gambit*

If you are dealt two low spades and you are passed the ♠Q and two high clubs or diamonds, you have no hope to slam if you also hold at least two low clubs and two low diamonds. If you hold no heart and are strong in the minors, however, then you might consider slam. Usually opponents will push spades to smoke out the Queen. These opponents hold ten spades among themselves, so why should they not push? But with ♠Q J x you have a fair chance, as seen in Deal 4.

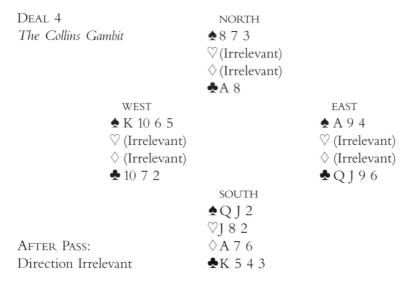

DEAL 4
*The Collins Gambit*

NORTH
♠8 7 3
♡ (Irrelevant)
◇ (Irrelevant)
♣A 8

WEST
♠ K 10 6 5
♡ (Irrelevant)
◇ (Irrelevant)
♣ 10 7 2

EAST
♠ A 9 4
♡ (Irrelevant)
◇ (Irrelevant)
♣ Q J 9 6

SOUTH
♠Q J 2
♡J 8 2
◇A 7 6
♣K 5 4 3

AFTER PASS:
Direction Irrelevant

The spade holdings and South's hand are critical. South's prospects to unload the ♠Q are poor. Five club leads or four diamond leads are a mad hope. South's hearts are futile for slam. The only hope is in the spade suit itself. North's ♣A wins trick one and North immediately leads his ♠8, which is ducked around to West's King. West returns his

---

*Named for Walter Collins of Hialeah, Florida.

♠10; North and East must follow low, and South wins with his Jack. South pauses and thinks, "North led a spade, denying the Ace or King poorly guarded. West ditched his King on the first round, then continued spades, denying an unprotected Ace. So West must have held at least King fourth. Eight spades have been played. If the Ace is dry in East, it can be speared; if protected, another spade lead will kill me anyway." So South leads his black witch, spearing East on his dry Ace! This spear-play try is not a lead-pipe cinch, for there is no guarantee that the Queen lead will drop the Ace. The try is based on inferences and deduction. South has nothing to lose. If he hesitates and switches, he may let East discard his ♠A if out of another suit. South must play for this chance on his holding.

Presume the same hand as above, but that the ♠J lies West and the ♠6 lies South. West would win the first spade lead with his King and lead his Jack. Next he would lead his ten and trap East. These repeated spade leads through are deadly to East.

Finally, if you hold the ♠Q with Ace or King and two low spades at most in a hand like South's above, you will probably get nailed. If the King fails to show after two spade leads you would do well to play the Collins Gambit. Lead your ♠Q and hold your breath; pray for the Ace or King to come down. After all, you cannot win all the time, but quitters *never* win. So dig in and fight it out!

## Passes to the Right

About once in six deals you will be served ♠A Q or ♠K Q with two or fewer low spades: typically ♠A Q 6 3 or K Q 10 7 or A Q 6 or K Q 8, etc. Normally you would pass the Queen and Ace or King to your RHO and think nothing about it, being happy to be rid of her and consoled to know where she is. Occasionally you may be forced to keep all of ♠A Q x x or ♠K Q x x for tactical reasons arising from the condition of other suits or the possibility of slam, to be discussed later. With ♠A Q x or ♠K Q x, you should normally pass both honors—a must on a pass to left or directly across unless you have good slam material. However, with the pass to *right* there is one exception. It is not necessary to pass both honors, only the Queen! Why? You know that your RHO has the Queen, so no enemy spade lead can spear you with ♠A x or ♠K x. You are South; with pass to right, you are dealt ♠A Q x. Pass the Queen and two nonspade cards. If North leads a spade, you can play your Ace, assuming, of course, that East does not drop the

Queen before you play. If West leads a spade, you enjoy the safety of fourth position, last to play.

Another advantage of keeping the ♠A K or ♠K x and passing the ♠Q to RHO is that it frees you to pass another card instead of the Ace or King, such as a high club or diamond or that standard defense to stop a possible slam, a low or middle heart. Remember that this position applies only to the pass to the *right*. With the pass left or across and ♠A Q x x or ♠K Q x x or especially ♠A Q x or ♠K Q x, pass both honors.

If you are dealt ♠A Q or ♠K Q dry (i.e., with no other spade) a good bluff pass to right is the Queen only! Now your RHO with the Queen does not know that he can spear you, unless you hold your hand too low. Remember the old adage, "As ye show, so shall they peep"!

*If you apply all that you have read in this section, your scores will improve.* Later I will illustrate where a chap had the ♠Q singleton after the pass, with no hope for a slam, yet ate fewer than five points! And no one else at his table made a go for slam either. I do not guarantee complete success—you will have unlucky stretches—but I do promise lower scores. Good luck!

## MORE ON SPADES

Examine below the four-card spade holdings before the pass:

| | | | | |
|---|---|---|---|---|
| HAND A | ♠Q J 5 3 | ♡A 5 | ◇Q 10 | ♣K J 8 6 |
| HAND B | ♠Q J 5 3 | ♡A 5 | ◇Q 3 2 | ♣K J 4 3 |

With Hand A, if you pass your ♣Q and two diamonds or two clubs, you will still be blocked in the minor suits. Probably you will absorb the ♠Q on either bad minor. But with Hand B you have a marked difference, *low minor-suit cards.* They allow more freedom for the pass. We advise the following:

With Hand A, pass the ♡A 5 and the ◇10. If a heart is not passed to you, your chances for slam are good. When you get on lead, run the minor suits. You may be able to get spade discards. If a heart is passed to you, lead it as soon as legal.

With Hand B, pass the ♡A 5 and the ♠Q. This may give your opponent a slam but you must risk it, or else you may eat 17 points or more if your ♠Q is smoked out. Play your high club on the first lead.

You will be reasonably safe for the remainder of the hand, barring bad breaks. To sum up:

(1) If Queen fifth or more spades (including A Q x x x and K Q x x x) were dealt to you, keep the Queen.

(2) But with ♠Q x x x, use judgment. A safer holding is ♠ A Q J 10, rather than ♠Q 7 5 2. The weakest holding is Queen and three low. Pass her then, unless other suits are poor in exit cards, as in Hand A above.

(3) Finally, with ♠Q x x or ♠Q x or ♠Q dry, pass her. See the section, "Passes to the Right," above.

(4) Remember, it is always nice to have control of the Queen, but you must be able to stop the opponents from driving it out. The quality of your "backers" (supporting spades) is so critical.

## The Rubin Maneuver*

Before the pass, Rubin holds:

♠A Q J 10 9 3   ♡K 6 3   ◇Q 5   ♣A J

He is passing to his LHO, who has the highest score toward game. Rubin passes the ♠Q (!), the ♡6, and the ♣J. He wins with the ♣A and leads his ♠J. After the ♠K falls, our strategist gets in again and smokes out the ♠Q. This caper is called the Rubin Maneuver. I think that it is risky, but it may be worth a try if you are well ahead and want to gamble. Do not try it on minor-suit blocking cards or you may get back your ♠Q sooner than you expect.

This is one of the two "Depravation" plays in Hearts. A lot of players do not like becoming victims of this Maneuver! However, it is a perfectly legal play, and often considered good strategy if you are trying to aim for a particular player. It can be very effective if you are the low player in a game and want to push the high player "over the top" thus ensuring a win.

## The Rosner Suicide Pass†

Before the pass, Rosner holds:

♠Q 5   ♡K 7 6 3   ◇A J 5   ♣K J 7 4

* Named for Steve Rubin of Framingham, Mass.
† Named for Amelia Rosner of New York City.

She passes the ♠Q 5(!) and the ♡7 or a high diamond. If the dry ♠A or K is passed to her, she will fetch the Queen anyway unless led up to. So what difference does it make if she keeps the ♠5? If someone smokes spades through her, the five will be useless to stop the pushes. A variation is to pass the ♠A x or ♠K x when dealt them doubleton. Rosner says, "If a dry ♠Q is passed to you, one spade guard will not make that much difference." This tactic has some merit, but we recommend that any low spade be kept and instead a dangerous card in another suit be passed. (A variation of the Rosner strategy is to pass the singleton ♠J, ♠10, or ♠9.)

I am not an advocate of the pass of a low spade, as I firmly believe that any spade lower than the Queen is just too valuable to release. Besides, the pass of a middle heart or high card in a minor suit is a much better strategy. Yet, there are times voiding the spade can provide an opportunity to discard other suits. After all, a singleton Jack or ten is probably useless, and can throw you into the lead at a critical time.

*HOT TIP—After the pass, you hold* Q x of spades, four clubs, four diamonds, and three middle or high hearts. The Moon is out of the question. You are in second or third place in a close game. You have little hope of dumping the Lady! Try to duck the first club, saving a high card for later. If a spade is led, take your Queen immediately! Now cash the high club and then lead your other spade. This will give you a chance to unload a high heart or two. This applies only to the holding of the Queen and one small backer. If you have 2 or more supporting spades, you should duck leads in this suit—hoping to catch the Ace or King if you are lucky! The idea is to escape the hand for thirteen or fourteen points. This strategy was first innovated by Richard Freedman of Toronto, Canada, and holding the damage to thirteen points is called "taking a Freedman Queen."

## Holding of Poorly Guarded Ace or King

An agonizing decision is what to pass when dealt ♠A x x or K x x. With Ace or King doubleton, pass the honor (high card), rarely both cards as in the Rosner Suicide Pass. Some players like to keep ♠A x x or K x x in order to guard against a Queen pass, which, if it occurs, gives the ♠A Q x x or K Q x x. Other players hope for a lead up to ♠A x x or K x x held by the fourth hand. I think that keeping the high spade is risky. Only once in three times will your passer be dealt the ♠Q and then not always will he pass her to you. Even if you end with

Ace-Queen or King fourth, your Queen is poorly guarded and spades must split 4-3-3-3 to avoid a smokeout of your Queen. Possibly you might spear a top spade or discard the Queen. More importantly, you may be led through or toward two or three times, and, if you do not hold the Queen, she will land in your trick pile. I have seen ♠A x x and K x x get speared often; so it is better to pass the Ace or King here.

The best pass from ♠A K x x is to split, to pass the Ace and keep the King, leaving you with only one headache. With a good hand you might pass both top spades. With decent hearts, try voiding clubs and one top spade. If no club and no ♠Q is passed to you, you can discard the high spade on trick one. But with ♠A x x x or K x x x, keep the high spade. Rarely will you get speared. You will have a better chance to play or discard the high spade, thanks to your extra low card. If you pass the ♠A or ♠K from A x x or K x x and receive the Queen, consider the Collins Gambit, especially when you have no chance to discard her. This is especially advisable with the pass across. If your LHO leads spades twice and a top honor fails to show, get on lead quickly and lead your ♠Q. Nine times out of ten she will spear a dry Ace or King. Why? Because your LHO will rarely underlead an Ace or King without many spades, and your across-table opponent probably passed the Queen from ♠Q x x. More likely the ♠A or ♠K will appear on the second spade lead, and sometimes your third-round Queen lead will crash both Ace and King, the double spear! The ♠A K Q all on one trick is beautiful to all—except the ♠A holder!

## The "Scatter Pass" Technique

The scatter pass certainly creates some interesting possibilities relating to the spade suit. If you are dealt A x x or K x x, simply pass the high spade to the right. Then you will have a decent chance of parking the Queen, if she is passed to you. Of course, this depends on the distribution of the suit. If you are dealt A Q x (x) or K Q x (x), pass the Queen (only) to the right and await developments. A real devilish play (and variation with this holding), is the pass of the Ace or King to the player across from you and the Queen to the right. The idea here is to "nail" the person opposite you, by leading through his high spade, and hoping that he has to go up with the Ace or King—catching the Queen! Remember, all does not go according to plan, and you may get your Queen back rather quickly, especially if your other suits are weak! Finally, another good strategy which occasionally works with all passing schemes, is the pass of the Ace of clubs to the left hand opponent. If you have the Ace or King of spades, the Ace of clubs may be taken on trick one and you may get a "free" lead to your high spade. Lastly, don't forget the defensive pass of that middle heart, as a Moonshot deterrent!

## The Overloaded-Queen Syndrome

The overloaded-Queen syndrome exists when you hold, for example, ♠A Q 10 8 7 6, a great broken spade suit with the Queen and no way to avoid eating her or to make slam in the endgame. (The danger is that, after your "exit" cards are stripped, you will be thrown in and trapped on lead.) An extreme remedy is the Rubin Maneuver; a more effective one is proper play. *This avoidance often wins unless the hand is so hopeless that even Houdini cannot escape.*

Suppose that after the pass you are looking at:

♠A Q J 9 7 6    ♡K 6 5    ◇A 3    ♣A K

This is a most interesting hand. If you cash your ♣A K and then your ◇A 3, a spade return will place you in a difficult bind. Now you must try to strip spades and hope that heart discards are favorable. Why go through all this grief?

Play the ♣A on trick one and immediately play the ♠9. If the King appears, all is well. Otherwise, take any return high (a spade lead makes life easy), and proceed to strip spades, until a heart is played. Now cash the ♡K and exit with ♡6. The key card here is the ◇3. Unless there are ridiculous distributions, you should be able to strip hearts and clubs, if necessary, and escape with the ◇3.

In summary, the management of spades is the key to success. You must learn to recognize spade danger or trouble, and act accordingly. Because everything revolves around the Queen of spades, you should try to keep her—if you possibly can. But she is better passed if you do not have adequate support. Similarly, the Ace and King are problems if not sufficiently guarded. Review the illustrated examples and apply the techniques and principles in your game.

# Chapter Five
# PLANNING YOUR PLAY

## PLANNING AND STRATEGY

After the pass has been made and the deuce of clubs led, you're ready to go. We have already discussed the proper strategy for handling the spade suit, and what to do if you hold the Queen of spades.

If you don't have the Queen, and the player who wins the first trick doesn't play spades, it can be assumed that he has spade problems. He also may be planning to strip his hand in preparation for the so called "grand exit" (stripping the hands of all opponents and then playing a key exit or "out" card). In any event, his first objective will be to park his Queen of spades, and you can rest assured that he will lead his shortest minor suit. Occasionally, he will try to get his LHO on the lead—in a desperate hope to have the Ace or King of spades led through. Your mission should be to lead low spades repeatedly so as to smoke out the enemy Queen, or to make a safe escape by leading low cards in the minor suits.

Hearts is a game of collusion. Temporary "partnerships" are often formed for these objectives:

(1) Smoking out the Queen of spades.
(2) Stopping a potential slam.

(3) Dumping the Queen of spades on the person who has the low score.

(4) Protecting the person with the high score (in order to prolong the game, especially if you are in third place).

(5) Allowing a certain player to score slam, if the result does not hurt you.

You must be able to determine who might want to give you help at a given moment. If you have the low score, especially near the end of the game, you may find out what "three on one" is all about!

### HAND A    ♠J 3    ♡A 10 8 5 3    ◇A J 7 3    ♣A K

Now we offer three hands for play-plan analysis. In Hand A you win with the ♣A and lead the ♠J. If the ♠Q does not show and you play the ♠3, then you may be thrown back in via a club and you will have a ticklish decision in diamonds. So cash the ♣A K early. (An alternate, and inferior, plan is to attack the spades and hope for a club discard.) If on one you get the ♠Q, assume that you would have gotten her anyway since two opponents have all the low clubs. Next lead your ♠J. If spades or clubs are led a third time, you can pitch high diamonds (best) or shed hearts (acceptable). Cashing high no-point cards when you lack the ♠Q is called "clearing." If long in clubs, do not cash high cards so early.

### HAND B    ♠K Q 10 3    ♡J 4    ◇A 3    ♣A K 9 8 5

In Hand B your ♠Q is poorly guarded. Yet resist the temptation to play the ♣A at trick one. Instead, play your *nine!* Watch what spots appear. Take the expected spade return with your King if led up to, or duck with the ten if led through or toward. If clubs behave very well for you, you may make it. If you can win the next spade lead, do so; otherwise, if led through or toward, duck with your three. When you win a spade, hopefully a third or earlier spade lead, run clubs till they are exhausted and a heart is discarded. If hearts are held up, shift to the ◇A, then ◇3. If hearts are broken, cash your ◇A, then lead your ♡J. If this wins, play your last diamond and hope that whoever wins it has no spade left to lead. This hand, difficult to figure, depends much on discards. Another line of play is to win trick one with your ♣A and lead the ◇A, then ◇3, hoping for a diamond return. However, a black-suit return will put you in a tight spot and you may eat your own ♠Q. Opponents will observe that you have stripped diamonds.

HAND C    ♠A 4    ♡Q 10 8 5 3    ◊4    ♣A Q 8 6 3

Hand C illustrates a familiar frequent motif. If your opponent across the table leads the ♣2, try to duck to your LHO. Then he might lead a spade up to your Ace. Unless you know that the ♠Q is on your right, make sure to keep your RHO off lead. Unless you know that your OAT holds the ♠Q, do not leave him on lead at trick two. Your key tactic is to avoid having your ♠A led through. If forced to win the ♣2 lead, lead your dry diamond at once. This may give you a shot to pitch the top spade on the second diamond lead. Try to keep your ♣3 on at least the first two club leads. You may need it later for an emergency exit.

**HOT TIP:** *Always try to play cards passed to you as early and as comfortably as possible.* If you are passed two high diamonds or clubs, play them early, or else a crafty opponent will know that you hold such a card or cards, and in the middle or end game can hurt you.

## CONTROL CARDS (EXIT CARDS)

A "control card" is one that is impossible for an opponent to duck. Basic control cards are the ♠2, the red deuces, and the ♣3 (the ♣2 is an artificial lead card). As long as you hold a control card and carefully count its suit, you should have few worries. If you are dealt the ♣K Q 7 5 and fail to pass any, you stand an excellent chance of fetching the enemy-held ♠Q. But with ♣K Q 7 5 3 you are virtually untouchable, unless you flub. With ◊A K 10 5 4 you are in the same fix as with ♣K Q 7 5. But add that ◊2, and your diamonds are like the Rock of Gibraltar. This feature of the game lets you pass cards in other suits. Because hearts are usually led in the middlegame, your hearts are not as critical as either minor suit. Yet the player who *does have* the ♡2 has a big edge, especially if the ♠Q shows up late. The least important control is the ♠2. Spades are usually pushed early, yet sometimes the ♠2 furnishes a vital exit out of a tight spot.

## DUCKING

If you hold high and low cards of a red suit or clubs, our best advice is to play high early; save low cards for later ducks. The road of Hearts is strewn with the wreckage of hands where some unfortunate player tried to duck one lead too many—only to be locked on lead by his high cards in the end. Suppose you hold this hand:

♠J 10 5    ♡Q 10 4 3    ◊A 8 3    ♣K 8 4

Play your ♣K to trick one. If it wins, lead spades at once, the ♠J. If diamonds are led, step in with your Ace immediately and shift back to spades. Barring wild splits, you should be safe for the rest of the hand. If a low heart is led, play your Queen at once. If you try to be hoggish to avoid four points, your Queen may fetch another Queen, not the one you want! If you hold one exit card and two high cards of a suit, play your high card on the first round, then shift if possible or practical. If your bad suit is led again, play your second high card and pray. It does not pay to duck if you can play high with reasonable safety. Finally, if you hold a five-card or longer suit, duck if possible, especially on its control card and another low one.

## REMEMBERING SPOT CARDS

Make an effort to watch the cards played on every trick. This is as important as counting suits. If you hold the ◊3, and the deuce appears on the first or second trick, your three becomes exit control. Be wary of an opponent who tosses away a very low card, then shows up with higher cards in the same suit. As I said before, that player has moonlight in his eyes—he is slam-minded!

## THE ORIN JOHNSON MANEUVER

Tourney Hearts player Orin Johnson of San Diego, California, performed superbly in a tournament finals early in 1974. He was dealt a bad hand: no spade, ♡K 10 9, and minor-suit trash. He passed his hearts

♠A Q    ♡J    ◊A K Q 10 9 7    ♣A K J 5

only and received ♡J and ♠A Q, ending with the hand in the diagram. It was too bad that he got that dry ♡J. Maybe all might have laid off it and given Orin a chance for slam, but no chance. His opponents were not turkeys. Orin, nevertheless, made his famous Orin maneuver. First he ducked the ♣2 opening to the Queen. He won the spade return with his Ace. (Later he said that if he had been passed the ♠Q dry, he would have won the club opening and cashed all his minor-suit cards.) Now he ran all his clubs and diamonds, picking up ◇J x x. Two opponents voided their spades, including the King, in order to guard hearts. Orin's passer kept the ♡K and ♠2, good strategy. After trick eleven, Orin held the ♠Q and ♡J. He lost his Jack to the Ace and a heart return let him jettison his black lady. Some poor chap won trick 13 with his ♡3, catching the ♠Q! If this chap had discarded his last heart and kept spades, he might have survived, but who would expect to collect 15 black points with a lousy *three* of hearts?★

## THE VALUE OF SLAM

This hand should remind you of Orin's:

♠7     ♡K J 10 7     ◇A K 8 6     ♣A Q 10 8

If you normally pass the ♡J and two high clubs or diamonds, you may well eat the ♠Q on a bad minor. Those bad middle hearts threaten to stick you with ten points or more. The best pass is the ♡K J 10. This may let an opponent slam—better than eating 20 points yourself, for you will drag down with you *two other opponents,* who also lose slam. If you get stuck with the ♠Q, try to hold your carnage in hearts to a minimum. After all, 13 black points are better to eat than 20 to 25. This strategy is good, especially early in a Hearts-125 game. Consider all relative scores at the table. If available, go for Orin's maneuver.

How much is it worth to stop a slam? It depends on cumulative scores at the moment. In the early or middle hands 1–10 points are worthwhile, but 13 are too many. Try to get out as cheaply as possible, and do not duck an early heart lead with a high card, or two such leads with bottom low cards like ♡4 2 or ♡3 2.

---

★Orin was lucky, to be sure, as any expert defender would have reduced to the ♡A and a low spade. (The ♡3 was not a safe card.)

## THE SLAM ("MOON SHOT," "SMUDGE")

Most slams are made by mutual cooperation of two or more players. Sometimes a player who might be burned with many hearts and/or the Queen of spades will seek salvation by allowing another player to score slam. This is considered very good strategy.

Some slams are made because a certain player will not take just *one measly trick* containing four hearts. This is a case of pure greed. A more frustrating situation arises when a player has the audacity to duck the heart *he* passed to the person who subsequently scores slam.★

In certain cases, an opponent's discard of a key card will allow a person who had an otherwise hopeless hand to find himself suddenly in "slam city." Sometimes these errant discards are made under pressure and can be forgiven; in other cases, they are outright blunders and subject to the postmortem "rave reviews" of the other two players. It can be reasonably assumed that the player who has intentionally taken the spade Queen during the course of hand is preparing to go for Slam. It can be equally assumed that this player does not have a losing heart (unless of course you passed a heart to him)! Therefore, it does not make sense to keep a heart or two as a stopper. The only hope for a defense is to keep a high club or diamond or length in the side suit you suspect the "shooter" may have. Thus, as he "runs" the hand out, be sure you are on your toes! Sometimes, the "shooter" must take time to set up his hand, and this may give you vital information as to his distribution. Remember, one of the defenders must keep a heart, and another defender the high card in the potential "shooter's" side suit. If you have worthless cards in all suits, by all means keep a low heart! I have seen instances where everyone discards all of their hearts prematurely, and the Slam is given away! Your opponents become your partners when the time comes for stopping Slams! If you have to take the Queen of spades to stop a Shoot, it can be very damaging. However, it may be necessary to do so—ESPECIALLY if the "Shooter" is in a position to end the game and finish first!

A very good strategy is to "split" hearts. This is the technique of giving one heart to two different players. Of course, if you can take the first heart safely, you immediately remove any anxiety about

---

★I have seen cases where a player will pass the ♡Q (and keep the ♡K). Then the ♡Q will be led (after its holder has eaten the ♠Q). The person with the ♡K will *duck* and later ask, "Who had the ♡A?"

anyone else "shooting"! If one of your opponents takes the Spade Queen early in the hand, and then leads a middle Heart such as the ten, you are faced with a decision. If you have a higher heart, you may wish to take this trick. Often, it is the responsibility of the person who passed to the potential "shooter" to take the first heart lead. DON'T COUNT ON IT! There are Hearts "Hogs" out there who will not stop Moons! Use your best judgement, and if you can escape for four points, then grab that First heart trick, and remove all worry!

Finally, those slams do exist that are scored via sheer high-card strength massed in one hand (usually in top hearts and the Queen of spades). Nothing can be done here but to say, "Oh well—on to the next deal!" Slam is part of the game, and adds to its excitement.

# Chapter Six
# DEFENSIVE PLAY

## FORESIGHT

Defensive play is important. Awareness of many positions can help. For example, if you are passed bottom cards—deuces and treys, or three low hearts—beware of a lunar attempt (a moonshot or slam). If you see someone play a bottom card on the first lead of clubs or diamonds and later play a higher card, suspect him! Or if you pass the ♠A or ♠K to an opponent who does not play it in a safe position, keep your eyes peeled.

West was dealt a dry spade, always a dreadful thing, and he tried to void himself of diamonds. Since he held five clubs he reasoned that trying to void them was futile. Little did he know that this innocent maneuver would save the day. Meanwhile friend South, with lunar dust in his eyes, cleared his hand of obstacles to slam: *losers.* East failed to pass a low heart to South, and the path seemed clear. When West picked up South's pass, the ♡2 and ◇3 2, it smelled of a rat, a bit faintly at first. The smell grew stronger when South played his ♣3 to trick one and West cautiously played his nine. And the smell of slam really became overwhelming when South let West's ♠J hold the next trick. The ◇3 went to East's Jack, for South played his four. West realized that South must have no heart and had set up his hand to go for slam.* The

*If South had had a low heart, he would have cashed high minor-suit cards and stripped the hand routinely.

34

DEAL 5
*Foresight*

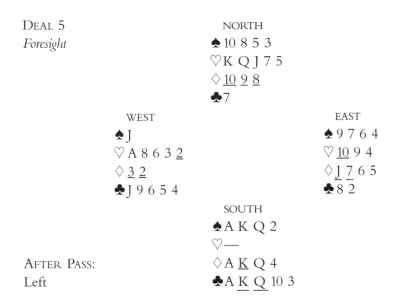

NORTH
♠ 10 8 5 3
♡ K Q J 7 5
♢ 10 9 8
♣ 7

WEST
♠ J
♡ A 8 6 3 2
♢ 3 2
♣ J 9 6 5 4

EAST
♠ 9 7 6 4
♡ 10 9 4
♢ J 7 6 5
♣ 8 2

SOUTH
♠ A K Q 2
♡ —
♢ A K Q 4
♣ A K Q 10 3

AFTER PASS:
Left

only chance for the defense was the well-guarded ♣J. South was quite happy and he took East's spade return with the Ace. Next he cashed his ♠K, and gurgled gleefully when he next laid down his ♠Q. Next he cashed his top diamonds, crowing, "I ought to get an Oscar for my performance." West quietly threw his low hearts on the spade and diamond tricks; and on the last diamond he jettisoned his ♡A. North and East groaned and showed looks of disgust. However, West knew that South would *never* have tried a moonshot if he had held hearts; and besides, South had tossed his ♣3 on trick one.* Now South cashed his ♣A K, drawing one heart each from North and East, low clubs and a wry smile from West. South, who had forgotten the guarded ♣J, still thought that he had made slam, and cashed his last two top clubs; and West grabbed the last trick with his last club, that well-preserved Jack. North had conveniently saved a heart to throw on the last trick. South wailed about his bad luck, but West's foresight had stopped South's slam.†

*Some sly players will fake a slam try with a losing heart. But no one will freely lead the ♡Q if holding a losing heart except on a spear try.
†South played like a drib to eat so many points. After losing a trick in each of his three suits, he should have tested clubs, to win a third round. If the ♣J had dropped in a favorable split of enemy clubs or someone had left the Jack unguarded, South's hand would have been solid for slam; or else South could have gotten out cheaply by losing trick twelve to the then dry ♣J, and on the forced heart return could have dumped his ♠Q to salvage at least 13 points.

## DEFENSE UNDER PRESSURE (THE PSEUDO-SQUEEZE)

Occasionally an opponent may try to demoralize you into believing that your position is hopeless or that you have no defense in a particular situation. Here South gave the impression that his hand was iron-clad, but East kept cool and saved the day with brilliant reasoning.

DEAL 6
*Defense Under*
*Pressure*

AFTER PASS:
Right

|  | NORTH | |
|---|---|---|
|  | ♠ 9 8 4 3 2 | |
|  | ♡ J 4 | |
|  | ◇ K 9 7 4 3 | |
|  | ♣ 3 | |
| WEST | | EAST |
| ♠ 5 | | ♠ A Q 7 6 |
| ♡ 8 7 5 3 2 | | ♡ K Q 10 9 6 |
| ◇ 10 8 6 5 2 | | ◇ J |
| ♣ K 10 | | ♣ 8 7 5 |
| | SOUTH | |
| | ♠ K J 10 | |
| | ♡ A | |
| | ◇ A Q | |
| | ♣ A Q J 9 6 4 2 | |

South was grateful to receive the ♣Q J 9 from West, who voided his clubs to get a spade discard (in the event that he might be passed a high spade by North). North instead unloaded his two high clubs and the ◇10. Note South's pass to East and his safe ♠K hold. With great clubs and the dry ♡A, South smelled slam. West won the ♣2 lead with his King and returned his ♠5. North ducked, East played a low spade, and South's Jack won. South led his ◇Q and North's King★ won, as East's Jack fell. North's ♠9 rode to South's ten after East ducked; West shed his last club. Had East played his ♠A, South would have unloaded his King, with a heart pitch from West a sure bet. Following this line, East's escape in clubs or hearts would have been futile, for South would have cashed both his diamond and heart Aces, cleared his ♠10, and buried East alive with the ♣4. But East ducked the second spade trick, and South was in. Therefore, he ran his clubs to this position:

★Rising with the King was an unnecessary risk, especially with his long suit.

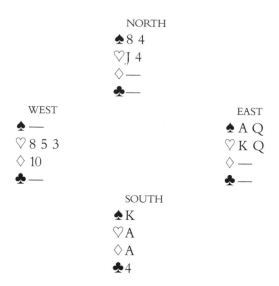

NORTH
♠ 8 4
♡ J 4
♢ —
♣ —

WEST
♠ —
♡ 8 5 3
♢ 10
♣ —

EAST
♠ A Q
♡ K Q
♢ —
♣ —

SOUTH
♠ K
♡ A
♢ A
♣ 4

Note that West and North had correctly saved hearts, and East kept the ♠A. From the holdings shown in the matrix, South cashed his red Aces; East chucked his ♡K Q. West and North each kept two hearts. Now South led his last club. East thought that he was being squeezed. If he cast his ♠A, he would set up South's King to score the slam. If he cast his ♠Q, it would seem to give South the card that he wanted. East thought it over once more. Of his two other opponents, surely each would have a heart left for the last trick. So East tossed his ♠Q. South's last card was the ♠K. This lost to East's Ace, which scooped heart discards from East's delighted fellow players. If East had parted with his ♠A on an early spade trick, or discarded it on a later club trick, he would have died accordingly. This deal is a good example of good reasoning in a difficult defensive position, considering the highly complicated nature of the hand.

## THE STRIP PLAY ("GRAND EXIT")

The strip play is a strategy executed by a player who holds the Queen of spades and a control card in another suit. This is often called the simple "grand exit."

The game plan is to protect the exit card or cards at all costs (even if it means taking hearts). The idea is to rid the hand of all potential "thrown-in" (forced entry) cards before executing the final escape with the control card that gets the hand out of the lead forever. Here is an example:

DEAL 7              NORTH

*The Grand Exit*

NORTH
♠ 7 4 3
♡ A 10 6 3
◇ K 9 8
♣ 10 7 5

WEST
♠ 10 9 5 2
♡ J 5 4
◇ J 10 4 2
♣ J 2

EAST
♠ 6
♡ Q 9 7
◇ 7 6 5 3
♣ A 9 6 4 3

SOUTH
♠ A K Q J 8
♡ K 8 2
◇ A Q
♣ K Q 8

AFTER PASS:
Direction Irrelevant

West opened with the ♣2, on which South correctly played the ♣8 after he saw the ♣A. East shifted to the ♠6, which South followed with the eightspot. West, who won with the ten, now continued with the nine, and South inserted the Ace, East having discarded a low heart. Momentarily South let spades dangle, and played the ◇Q. This fetched the King from North and the obvious spade shift.★ South, in full control now, cashed the K J of spades, extracting West's low spots, and two more hearts from East. Next he cashed the top clubs and the Ace of diamonds. Finally, he played the ♡K and sat back. If necessary he would take a few more hearts with the eight, but the heart deuce guaranteed safe passage for unloading his spade Queen. South thus saved at least 13 points by using the 'grand exit' strategy.

★If North had made the "off the wall" play of the ♡A, followed by a low heart, South would have dropped the ♡8 *first,* and would then have won the heart return with the King, retaining control.

## STRIP TECHNIQUE: THE BACKWARD STRIP

One essential element in a strip play is locating the ♠Q. If, through the pass or play inference, you know who holds her, this can help. The experienced player with the ♠Q after the pass will try to strip his minor suits so as to be able to unload her. Many hands occur with room to err. There is a right way and a wrong way to strip a hand. If opponents are alert, they can punish the player who uses the wrong technique. See the next deal:

DEAL 8
*The Backward Strip*

AFTER PASS:
Left

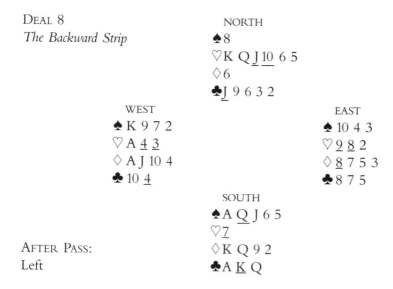

NORTH
♠8
♡K Q J 10 6 5
◇6
♣J 9 6 3 2

WEST
♠K 9 7 2
♡A 4 3
◇A J 10 4
♣10 4

EAST
♠10 4 3
♡9 8 2
◇8 7 5 3
♣8 7 5

SOUTH
♠A Q J 6 5
♡7
◇K Q 9 2
♣A K Q

### The Wrong Way

South's pass of the ♡4 3 and ♣4 alerted West to a slam try. However, East knew his way around Hearts tables, so West felt confident that East had passed a low heart to South.* So South quit his slam plan and stripped the hand *backwards!* He cashed his ♣A K Q; West discarded his ♠K. Next South led his ◇K, which West won with his Ace. Then West returned his ♠9. East played his ten and South won with his Jack. South now led his ◇Q, and when North hearted this trick, South abruptly shifted to the ♡7. West pounced on this with his Ace as South chortled and thanked West for the favor. West paused and deduced that South held the ♠Q because of:

*Now we can see the dampening effect on slams that the pass of a low heart creates.

(1) South's persistent high-club and diamond leads.
(2) South's failure to push spades.

Since the ♡7 was probably a singleton, South was most likely long in spades. Having not seen the ◇2 fall, West played his Jack first, drawing a heart from North and the nine from South; then West led his ◇4. This drew another heart from North, East's ◇3, and South's deuce. West smiled and led his ♠7. He could have exited with his ♡3, burying North alive, but he was after South. No matter how South played on spades, he would be dead. Actually he ducked the ♠7 and the deuce nailed him just in time for him to eat his Queen. If West had exited via his ♠2 instead of the ♠7, South could have turned the tables by taking his Ace and escaping via his six, throwing West in with his seven. But West was too smart to let South do this. At the outset South had intended to strip West of clubs and diamonds, then exit via the ◇2, but West stripped *South* of diamonds and then nailed him in spades.

Was this bad luck for South? The deal reminds me of the many times I heard an opponent wail about his bad luck when his own *bad play* did him in. Yet South could have played *the right way!*

## The Right Way

Suppose that the play proceeds as follows. South cashes his ♣A K Q and West discards his ♠K. Then South leads his *six of spades,* drawing the ten from East. East returns his ♠3, South wins with his Jack and cashes his ♠A, *drawing all enemy spades.* This ends phase one. North probably discards a heart on the second or third spade lead—it does not matter which. South still holds his *protected* ◇2. To trick seven, South leads his dry ♡7 and all correctly duck,★ or else South's task would be easy. South leads his ◇K and West plays his Jack. South leads his ◇Q, West dumps the ten, and North sheds a heart. West finally takes the ◇9 with his Ace and returns the four. This South easily ducks with his deuce. West now is all hearts, and South is easily able to unload his ♠Q. If West takes his ♡7 earlier, it gains nothing, except four fewer points for South. No matter how diamonds are played, the deuce lets South exit or duck the fourth round. If West discards a diamond instead of the ♠K on the third club lead, here *East* gets spiked on the fourth diamond lead with his ◇3 or ◇5. If diamonds split 4-3-3-3, South can

---

★East may choose to play his ♡9 in order to save his deuce, and shift to a diamond, depending on West's discard.

escape via his deuce on the third round. (South learns about the diamond split when North fails on the second round.) Finally, if diamonds are sour and West keeps his ♠K, the ♠Q may spear his King. West would be leading spades away from his King. South counts spades, hoping to knock the ♠Q and ♠K on the same trick.

## Strip Play—Advanced

We come to a more complex strip. In Deal 9, South seems to have only one exit card the ♣3, but he loses this early and transforms the deal into a lesson in psychology. In this deal the play is excellent.

East's ♣2 goes to South's three and West's Queen. South can afford to give up this control card because the key card in this deal is the ♡Q.

While stripping, South can play on his opponents' fear of slam. West returns a spade and South draws all enemy spades in four rounds. North sheds two hearts and a club, and East releases his ♣J on the fourth spade. North's early heart discards do not affect the play, for later he would be forced to discard hearts on the diamond run. Now South wins with his two top clubs, and West unloads his ◇10. Finally, South wins four diamond tricks while East and West pitch low hearts; and South leads his dry ♡Q. If she wins, South's ♠Q scores slam. So West takes the ♡Q with his Ace, and on the next trick South unloads his ♠Q. South escapes with six points.

Let us examine further alternatives.

DEAL 9
*The Advanced Strip*

NORTH
♠ J
♡ 7 6 5 4
◇ 7 6 5 2
♣ 9 7 6 5

WEST
♠ 9 8 7 6
♡ A J 10 3
◇ 10 4 3
♣ Q 8

EAST
♠ 4 3 2
♡ K 9 8 2
◇ J 9
♣ J 10 4 2

SOUTH
♠ A K Q 10 5
♡ Q
◇ A K Q 8
♣ A K 3

AFTER PASS:
Left

(1) If South leads his ♡Q before running diamonds, after North plays a heart on a spade trick, a diamond return would kill South.

(2) If South wins trick one in order to keep his ♣3, again the strip is partial only. First, if South plays his ♣K, then ♣3, a heart goes on the three, and an opponent wins and then shifts to a spade to rook South for 25 beautiful black points, unless West grabs the ♡Q with his Ace. Secondly, if South saves his ♣3, then runs spades and diamonds, he would make no slam threat. If opponents defend properly, South would probably take ten hearts and barely escape from the ♠Q.

(3) All other lines fail for South. We leave them for you to solve.

The original line is sound against any defense. South would fail only if an opponent holds five or more spades. Even so, *that* opponent must take trick twelve. This fine example combines advanced one-exit strip play with taking advantage of one's opponents' fear of a successful slam try.

## "WITH A LITTLE BIT OF LUCK": THE EVANS MOON

Sandy Evans, formerly of Boston, attended many of the early tournaments. Her name became synonymous with a type of slam: the "Evans Moon." I was the victim of one of these slams; the hand is still quite vivid (see Deal 10).

Sandy, playing South, was quite shocked to receive the Queen of spades *and* the Ace and King of hearts. Her hand, which had been reasonably safe before the pass, now looked rather hopeless. The spade Queen was weakly supported and the heart suit was ripe for gathering at least eight points, probably more.

Meanwhile, West was licking his chops at the prospect of driving out the spade Queen. The ♣A was the winner of trick one, after which a predictable shift to spades followed. This drew the Jack from West. Next he led the ten and finally the five, to which North pitched the ◇K and East a club.

Sandy commented that there should be a reduced penalty if you are forced to eat the spade Queen "shorthanded." After all, this card might be passed to you when you hold inadequate support.

The chance of a 4-3-3-3 heart distribution was poor, but the hand was a lost cause anyway. So Sandy plunked down the ♡A K Q. Twelve

DEAL 10
*The Evans Moon*

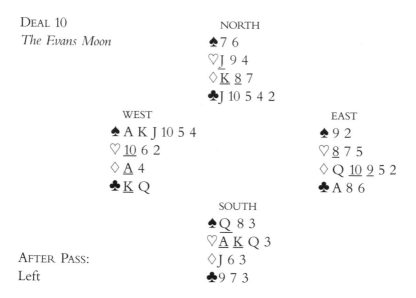

NORTH
♠ 7 6
♡ J 9 4
◇ K 8̲ 7
♣ J 10 5 4 2

WEST
♠ A K J 10 5 4
♡ 1̲0̲ 6 2
◇ A̲ 4
♣ K Q

EAST
♠ 9 2
♡ 8̲ 7 5
◇ Q 1̲0̲ 9̲ 5 2
♣ A 8 6

SOUTH
♠ Q̲ 8 3
♡ A̲ K Q 3
◇ J 6 3
♣ 9 7 3

AFTER PASS:
Left

hearts later, the three was a "thirteener," and, when it hit the table, Sandy was "on the moon"! In two years of tournament competition, Sandy made at least five of these Evans Moons. (Opposite of the Evans Moon is the "Rosner Split," in which a player holding ♡A K Q J x x x eats the ♠Q and discovers that someone holds ♡10 x x x x—enough to kill the slam!)

Yes, there is luck in Hearts and you do need occasional breaks. However, the player who masters the finer points of the game and learns to "read" his opponents' plays will win quite consistently.

## THE ENDPLAY

This term is taken from bridge. Basically, a player on lead strips or eliminates key cards. Then he throws an opponent in—who must make a favorable return. In this hand, West applies a similar technique. His precision play is rewarded with a slam.

No one enjoys having to absorb 26 points at any time; however, if you are a victim of brilliant play, I suppose it may be a bit easier to swallow. Watch this technique:

DEAL 11
*The Endplay*

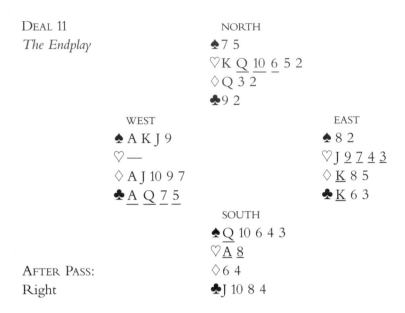

NORTH
♠7 5
♡K Q 10 6 5 2
◇Q 3 2
♣9 2

WEST
♠A K J 9
♡—
◇A J 10 9 7
♣A Q 7 5

EAST
♠8 2
♡J 9 7 4 3
◇K 8 5
♣K 6 3

SOUTH
♠Q 10 6 4 3
♡A 8
◇6 4
♣J 10 8 4

AFTER PASS:
Right

The ♣2 opening lead was taken by the King (South played the ten and West ducked with the seven). East's ♠8 was ducked by South and West's nine held. The ◇J shift was covered with the Queen and King, and a low spot by South. East played his remaining spade and West knew that South had the Queen. The Jack of spades held accordingly (an example of a "finesse"), and West now paused for thought. If the club suit was 4-3-3-3, the Jack would drop doubleton and the slam would roll home.

In Hearts, the percentages are *not* comparable to those of bridge (because of the pass feature). Therefore, in order to cater to the more likely 4-4-3-2 distribution, West played his low club and breathed a sigh of relief when North and East followed. (Note: A five-card stack in any hand would have been fatal. This, however, was unlikely since the spots on the first trick were the deuce, the King, and the ten.)

It did not matter who won this trick. The return of any suit (hearts could not be led since the suit had not been played or discarded) would be won by West's hand, and that was that.

It should be observed that West did not fall into the trap of leading the A Q of clubs and committing himself to the hope of a 4-3-3-3 break. Equally grievous would have been the overconfident play of the diamond suit. This would have fetched the spade Queen and the same club problem.★ Give credit to West for his well-played slam and his analysis of the distribution possibilities.

## ENDGAME POSITIONS

The term "endgame" is borrowed from chess. It indicates the stage of play when most of the pieces have been exchanged and, thus, when the board is relatively clear. In Hearts, the reference is to the stage of the hand in which each player holds fewer than six cards. Often, the hand is at a critical point where the outcome will be decided by one key play. Let us examine the seemingly simply situation below:

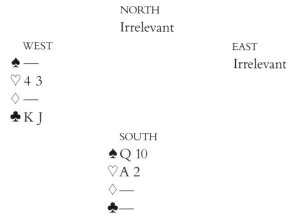

Hearts have been distributed evenly, and there is no slam threat. North and East hold safe clubs and diamonds, with no chance of obtaining the lead. West's clubs are winners. South holds the remaining two spades. Only four hearts are left, divided between South and West. Finally, South is on lead.

The question for South is this: are the two remaining hearts located in the *same hand,* or are they divided between *two hands?* Note that the Ace is the master (highest) card of the suit, and the deuce is the control (lowest) card. If the Ace is led and the 4 3 are *separated,* they will fall *under* the Ace, and South will be stuck with the good deuce, and will be forced to absorb the ♠Q. On the other side of the coin, if the

---

★Anyone would have simply led a heart and the slam would have been dead.

two cards are together, and the Ace is played, then the deuce will provide a perfect exit.

How can South be sure which way to play? In most cases, he would simply guess, and hope that he was right. Here, he has an additional chance. The play of the "good" ♠10 will place West in the hot seat. West may find it hard to resist discarding one of the hearts. Now South will have an accurate count on the suit, and his control card bails him out of the hand. Of course, West may choose to dump a club and force South to guess the heart suit. But the additional chance costs South nothing and may save him some grief.

Obviously, if the ♠Q is in another hand, South must make his heart choice rather quickly (especially if he holds winners in another suit).

Although somewhat basic, this is one of the more difficult plays in Hearts. It appears rather frequently, and can lead to a very ticklish situation especially if the spade Queen has NOT been played. Leading a side suit may result in the discard of BOTH of the cards in question or worse yet—the discard of the nasty Queen on you! The ideal situation is to have a sure escape card in the side suit, followed by the lead of your questionable suit, preferably from your left hand opponent! I have seen this theme occur within the Spade suit, itself. There are times when you have to be lucky, and there are other times when hard work can really pay off.

# Chapter Seven
# PSYCHOLOGY IN HEARTS

Like bridge, the game of Hearts embodies much of life. It brings to the card table so much brightness and shadow from the outside world, including a perfect dreamland for escape, quietude, and relaxation. Here one can find an outlet for self-expression. This is one reason for the success of Hearts. Here, at the Hearts table, the most tyrannical of personalities can try to express his need to dominate. The meekest individual can surmount all shyness and conquer his opponents with a well-planned slam or magnificent defense play. The spirit of the game arises from its setting for competition. Each table is a miniature battlefield. Here, every few minutes, one can taste hope and fear, victory and defeat. If one is shrewd, each early loss can be balanced by a later triumph—and the last one is the sweetest.

A knowledge of basic mathematics is helpful. More important are memory and concentration. Nothing can be more frustrating than to lose track of key cards or to lead a thirteener and catch the ♠Q. Concentration is the key to success. It requires effort, a low price for winning. Expert tournament Hearts demands precise memory, understanding, and play technique. The fluctuating luck of the deal tends to be equalized as more and more hands are played. In several deals, one key play can spell success or failure. Experience has proven that the consistent winners in tournament and social Hearts are not always those who pull off the most spectacular or complex plays. In many cases, victory goes to those who make the fewest mistakes in simple positions. Advanced technique helps occasionally, yet steady application of fundamentals usually decides the outcome.

An important part of judgment is a knowledge of psychology. All positions at the table are shaped by the four individual players. Each player should consider the mental processes of the others. Anticipating the play is part of technique. Some players are aggressive, for they think that they can go for slam every time; others are cautious and avoid abnormal play; still others are nervous and unsure. The man who plays his opponents as well as the cards will often be the victor. Learning to adjust to the psychological conditions of every position is part of the game.

In Hearts, the real psychology revolves around the threat that someone may score slam in every hand. Imagine the game without slams! Every hand would be an exercise in ducking everything in sight! High cards would become useless, and a strange game of low-card, no-trump whist would be created.

Now we can understand why Hearts has the deadly power of the Queen of spades, the pass of three cards, and a myriad of complicated and exciting strategies.

The following deals will illustrate the place of psychology in Hearts. Because the human element is woven as much into Hearts as into bridge, the personality factor comes to the fore many times during play. Some of the following illustrated positions are rare; they may never occur in actual play. Yet deals with positions similar to those illustrated here may appear in your games. Do not try to remember the hands card by card. Familiarize yourself with technique. It will go a long way to help you improve your play. Lastly, keep in mind that Hearts is only a game. Have fun while you play!

## THE HOG

In many Hearts groups one player refuses to pass no-slam insurance, *a low heart.* He tries to duck all high-card leads early, and he leaves to his opponents the dirty work of stopping slams. Most hogs usually get their due in situations like the one in Deal 12.

At first look, South thought that his hand was hopeless, then he thought, "Maybe I will be lucky to escape with ten hearts, if I can

DEAL 12
*The Hog*

AFTER PASS:
Across

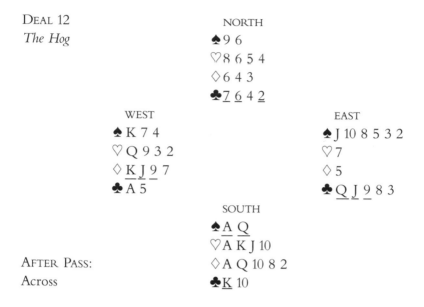

NORTH
♠ 9 6
♡ 8 6 5 4
◇ 6 4 3
♣ 7 6 4 2

WEST
♠ K 7 4
♡ Q 9 3 2
◇ K J 9 7
♣ A 5

EAST
♠ J 10 8 5 3 2
♡ 7
◇ 5
♣ Q J 9 8 3

SOUTH
♠ A Q
♡ A K J 10
◇ A Q 10 8 2
♣ K 10

dump the ♠Q on the third club trick." So he gave it the old try. Hog West took the opening club lead with his Ace and at once returned his ♣5, hoping to ditch his ♠K on another club lead. South had saved his ♣K for the second round. South now had to exit in diamonds but those high cards seemed discouraging. South led his ◇A, drawing the hog's King. South cashed his ◇Q and the hog tossed in his Jack (East discarded the ♡7). Then the ten drew Hog's nine and North's last diamond. Abruptly South switched plays. He kept his ◇2 for possible later exit and led his ♡J. Hog ducked this and ducked the ♡10 next. South led his ♠A and Hog threw his King as he snorted, "I do not want to eat that Queen!" The ◇8 extracted Hog's seven, and the ♡A K and ◇2 won the balance to score slam. East and North, with sure-zero hands, each swallowed twenty-six black points. Hog, who suffered the same fate, cursed his bad luck for his lousy hand and South's "icy" slam. East and North glared while South hid his grin.

**MORAL:** It is safe to remain quiet after you let an opponent score slam that you could have prevented. Lest opponents discover the true situation, quickly change the subject to avoid a postmortem!

## FEAR OF SLAM

DEAL 13                              NORTH
*Fear of Slam*                       ♠9 8 5
                                     ♡K 9 7 4
                                     ◇9 7 3
                                     ♣A 10 5

     WEST                                 EAST
   ♠A 7 2                               ♠J 3
   ♡J 5                                 ♡A Q 8 6 2
   ◇8 6 5 2                           ◇Q
   ♣9 6 3 2                           ♣K Q J 8 4

                     SOUTH
                     ♠K Q 10 6 4
                     ♡10 3
AFTER PASS:          ◇A K J 10 4
Left                    ♣7

    The ♣2 went to North's Ace; North shifted to the ♠9, which went to the Jack and West's Ace. West's ♠7 return went to South's ten. South then won five diamond tricks. Opponents were reluctant to break (discard) hearts lest South exit via a heart, so West shed a club and North two clubs and East dumped all four of his remaining clubs. Noting discards, South led his ♠K, and East, now all hearts, had to shed one, the Queen. Having stripped diamonds and spades, South led his ♡10, and West rose with his Jack, which North and East ducked. West confidently led his ♡5, but it drew the four, the trey, and the deuce—and an expression of pain. The ♣3 drew high hearts from North and East, and the well-preserved ♠Q. It seemed unfortunate for West that he had to eat twenty-five black points with his excellent hand, but that is the way the pasteboards plopped. Perhaps, however, West tried heroics unnecessarily. Sometimes a player will want to capture a heart purposely in order to lead a high heart, hoping to induce a patriotic opponent to take it. Usually a good policy is to take no chance and capture this sort of lead. But there is an unwritten law that the *passer* is responsible for stopping the potential slam of his receiver. Suppose East hold:

        ♠J 10 9 5    ♡K Q 7 3    ◇A K    ♣J 8 3

With pass left, East should pass to South the ◇A K and ♡Q. Later, when South plays his ♡Q, East should rise with his King, then exit via his ♡3 or ♣3. Sometimes a player hogs by ducking his pass-receiver's heart lead. This is like buying an insurance policy and failing to cash it. Of course, no rule says that you *must* take your insurance pass, but your opponents might not be too happy, especially if the aggressor slams as a result of your duck. In Deal 13, above, West should have tossed his ♡J on a diamond lead. The Jack has no value here. Then, when South led his ♡10, West could have played his five, his last heart, leaving him safe. West's chance to be a slam-stopping hero and eat twenty-five black points made no sense here.

## THE PHONY SMOKE

In Deal 14, south had passed the ♠K, ♡10, and ◇K to West. South would have done well to keep his ♠K with ♣J 10 9, but feared being trapped on lead with such high spades. Meanwhile, East had passed the ♠A Q and ♡K to South.

DEAL 14
*The Phony Smoke*

|  | NORTH | |
|---|---|---|
|  | ♠8 4 | |
|  | ♡J 9 4 3 | |
|  | ◇A 8 2 | |
|  | ♣Q 9 3 2 | |
| WEST | | EAST |
| ♠ K 7 6 3 | | ♠ 5 2 |
| ♡ 10 5 2 | | ♡ A 7 6 |
| ◇ K 5 4 3 | | ◇ 9 7 6 |
| ♣ 6 4 | | ♣ K J 10 8 7 |
|  | SOUTH | |
|  | ♠A Q J 10 9 | |
|  | ♡K Q 8 | |
|  | ◇Q J 10 | |
|  | ♣A 5 | |

AFTER PASS:
Left

South looked at his new hand and knew that he was in trouble. The ♠A Q was protected but his middle spades were high. Stripping black suits would be a waste of time, for sooner or later the diamond suit would be a killer; then he would be forced to eat his ♠Q.*

But South had a chance. West did not know that South had the ♠Q, but South *did know* that West had the ♠K. Now if West had some length in spades and spades split evenly. . . . South grabbed trick one with his ♣A, and unhesitatingly led his ♠J. West *did* hesitate, thought a bit, and played his ♠7. Next South led his ♠10, West again followed low, and South prayed hard that North and East each held one more spade, as they in fact did. So South, suppressing his smile, pushed his ♠9; West groaned, gazed at the ceiling, and ducked, expecting to see the smoked-out Queen drop from North or East. But both cast diamonds and West winced. South led his ♠Q, spearing West's King.

East commented on South's foxy caper and North chortled a bit. West muttered something about its being sunny on the beach. Later South won a trick with his ♡K, but escaped with only four black points.

**MORAL:** If you have the protected ♠Q and you know where the ♠A or ♠K is (except if it is with your RHO), and your minor suits are weak, try leading a middle spade, such as the Jack or ten. If the Ace or King holder ducks, try a low spade lead again, and count, and count, and count!

## THE FALSE CARD

In Deal 15, South felt stranded with the ♠Q 10 doubleton, and probably too many hearts. A slam was remote unless one opponent held ♡Q J dry. The only chance was to get a diamond lead, but surely opponents would push spades at once. A ray of hope was that the player who took trick one might hold the ♠A or ♠K only once or twice guarded. This would discourage an instant spade lead. So West led his ♣2, North rose with his Ace, East played his seven, and South tossed his *three* without the slightest expression. There must be something about seeing the ♣3 fall on trick one. North read South for a single-ton club and at least two or three diamonds. North himself, with his shaky spades, feared spade leads through his Ace. So he led his ◇J, keeping his deuce for later exit. East ducked high with his ten and South

---

*Note that, with its lack of low cards, the heart suit offers little relief. Any heart lead will be taken high, and a low heart return will "stuff in" South.

cast off his ♠Q without emotion. West ducked, and poor North was darted and shocked. When South later played four more clubs, North knew that he had been hornswoggled.

DEAL 15
*The False Card*

|  | NORTH | |
|---|---|---|
|  | ♠A 6 3 | |
|  | ♡Q 3 | |
|  | ◇A J 4 2 | |
|  | ♣A J 9 8 | |
| WEST | | EAST |
| ♠K 9 5 4 | | ♠J 8 7 2 |
| ♡5 2 | | ♡J 7 6 |
| ◇K 9 8 7 3 | | ◇Q 10 6 5 |
| ♣6 2 | | ♣7 4 |
|  | SOUTH | |
|  | ♠Q 10 | |
|  | ♡A K 10 9 8 4 | |
|  | ◇— | |
|  | ♣K Q 10 5 3 | |

AFTER PASS:
Left

**MORAL:** Do not always take cards at their face value. Although North can be forgiven for having fallen into a trap, he should have observed the spots on trick one. No *high* club appeared but the Ace. A spade lead by North would have been risky. But another club lead would have been sound in order to drive out the King or Queen. This might have drawn the ♠Q, but North would have had to absorb her anyway if South really had no club. (East or West might have led the ♣4 or ♣6, nailing North with his high clubs.) However, even if North *had* believed the false card, the ◇4 lead would have been better than the Jack lead. This would have preserved the ◇2, rid *North* of the lead,★ and, barring a weird diamond split, protected North from having to eat the ♠Q. It is difficult for *two* opponents to duck a four when you hold the deuce.

★As the cards lay, South's ♠Q dropped doubleton. In any event, North had a reasonable chance for a safe spade lead to his Ace in the fourth position.

## THE SLOW TORTURE

In a tournament (see Deal 16) South was dealt the ♡K Q dry, and he was reluctant to pass both these cards. So he kept the King and passed the Queen, the ♣A, and the ◇J to West. He was surprised to receive the ◇A Q 10, as he had expected to get a low heart. He had great spade length, but his diamonds and clubs were blockage. Yet he showed no concern that would tip opponents. West snapped up the opening ♣2 lead with his Ace, North depositing the King and South the ten. West, like South having plenty of spades, led his ♠10 with smoke aspirations. East shed his ◇K. South had mixed feelings; he laid off playing his five, so West continued with his nine. North heaved his ♣J and East dumped his ♡A, hoggishly. South won with his Jack and returned his ◇10, which went to West's Jack. The spade position was now clear and West disliked underleading (or leading) his ♠A K. So he exited via his ◇4, losing to the Queen. South cashed his ♣Q, then his ♣9, extracting West's low clubs and a heart and a diamond from North. South laid down his ◇A, drawing West's deuce, and South concealed a wince. The picture was complete. West had begun life with six spades, three diamonds, three clubs, and one heart—the Queen that had been passed to him. So South laid down his ♡K, scooping up

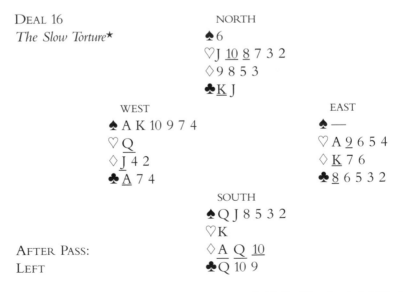

DEAL 16
*The Slow Torture*★

NORTH
♠6
♡J 10 8 7 3 2
◇9 8 5 3
♣K J

WEST
♠A K 10 9 7 4
♡Q
◇J 4 2
♣A 7 4

EAST
♠—
♡A 9 6 5 4
◇K 7 6
♣8 6 5 3 2

SOUTH
♠Q J 8 5 3 2
♡K

AFTER PASS:        ◇A Q 10
LEFT              ♣Q 10 9

★This is such an exquisite play! One of my players called it "walking the plank." The West player is so helpless!

West's dry Queen. Now South led his ♠8 and West rose with his King. (It would have done West no good to duck.) Poor West! He struggled like a fish on a hook, but he finally had to lead his ♠A, scoring twenty black points. This deal is a great demonstration of the value of counting.

The Microsoft Internet Gaming Zone (see appendix 5, which features the Internet) is a hotbed of Hearts activity! Upon entering the site, a host is usually available to help you find your preferred area. Lady "Mouser" was a great help to me when I was researching material for this section of the book! Another fine resource is the tournament coordinator, Julia Scott. Several outstanding players participate in many competitive events. The site is very well designed with several levels of play. Hungry Hearts "sharks" swim in the Zone waters! They appear with a variety of great nicknames (among my favorites are: "AmuseMe," "Horsedoctor," "PapaJack," "Nummy," "ChiefHearts," "Pea-UU," "Bullet," "Lowla," "Packerbabe," and "Eclectic.") There are lots of tournaments, a ratings ladder, and a plethora of private or invitational games. Once in a while, a truly memorable hand or stratagem will appear in a Zone game. One such play was observed by yours truly.

Dave Fanning (Hingham, MA) is one of the highest ranked players in the Zone. He has been near the top of the ladder ratings for some time, and has written columns for the Hearts Page. His precision approach to the game is impressive, and he has innovated some very clever stratagems. Observe one of these techniques, which I have chosen to call the "Fanman Maneuver." (Dave's nickname is "Fanman.")

♠Q 4     ♡K 10 7 4 3     ◇K 4     ♣A Q J 3

Fanman has a comfortable lead in a tournament game. The deuce of clubs is led by his left hand opponent, and Fanman takes the King with his Ace. His spade Queen is very vulnerable, and he knows that if he tries to strip diamonds, the opponents will start the spade suit. Therefore, he leads the spade four! This paints the picture that he does not hold the Queen. The opponents, who are anxious to "gang up" on Fanman, now become reluctant to drive spades. If they shift to clubs, Fanman will play high, and lead his diamond King. If it holds, he will clear the suit with the four. The opponents may accommodate him by trying a third round of diamonds, and it's "sayonara" to the nasty Queen!

Yes, there is no guarantee that this plan will work, but it offers a hope when standard play has little chance. (After all, the opponents have eleven spades between them and will attack the low-score person if they suspect he has a spade problem.) All in all, the "Fanman Maneuver" is a very neat tactic, and may bail you out of a desperate situation.

**CAUTION**—If you are not in first position, this maneuver is very risky, as you are implying that your hand is safe in spades. However, to quote Bob Dylan, "When you ain't got nothing, you got nothing to lose." (1965)

## THE TECHNICIAN

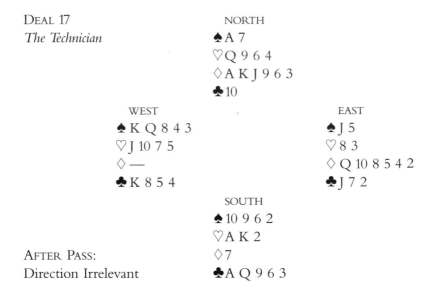

DEAL 17
*The Technician*

NORTH
♠ A 7
♡ Q 9 6 4
◇ A K J 9 6 3
♣ 10

WEST
♠ K Q 8 4 3
♡ J 10 7 5
◇ —
♣ K 8 5 4

EAST
♠ J 5
♡ 8 3
◇ Q 10 8 5 4 2
♣ J 7 2

SOUTH
♠ 10 9 6 2
♡ A K 2
◇ 7
♣ A Q 9 6 3

AFTER PASS:
Direction Irrelevant

South, who was an expert at the bridge table, and who prided himself on his play of the hand, demonstrated his technique. He calculated that he could dump one, and possibly both, of his high hearts on the second and third rounds of diamonds. This *could* save eight points.

He immediately played the ♣A on trick one and made the "scientific" play of the ◇7 on the next trick. This drew the ♠Q from West and two low diamonds from North and East. A bad day for science!

South expressed shock and disgust at the diamond distribution and fiercely watched West's discards for the rest of the hand (in case of a revoke). Twenty-one points later, the white flag went up.

We could argue a case for South's technique had he held North's cards (note the weakly protected spade Ace) and tried to get a spade discard on the diamond suit.

Here, however, the best play is the ♣A on trick one. West must not drop the ♣K, as he will need this card to improve his chances of stripping the suit.★ South now shifts to the ♠10, West playing low. North is virtually forced to play the ♠A (a finesse of sorts), unless he knows that East holds the ♠Q. The ♠7 then draws the ♠5, the ♠9, and the ♠K. West now reverts to clubs, first the ♣K and then the ♣5. North discards high hearts on both of these tricks, and thus splits the suit between two opponents, removing the threat of slam. South is thrown in with the third round of clubs, and pauses for thought. It appears that West is playing like a man who has never seen a diamond in his life! Otherwise, he would have cleared any singleton (or doubleton) diamond from his hand instead of the club suit. South may now exit in either black suit—throwing West on lead. West's desperate shift to hearts (after he removes his remaining black-suit cards—except the ♠Q) is taken by the Ace, followed by the King, and finally by the ♡2. West is buried alive with his ♠Q. And South escapes with nine points at most, depending on the previous discards. This is certainly a mathematically and *scientifically* superior result.

South needs a bit of luck to survive this hand, as he can never be 100 percent sure that West is *really* void of diamonds. However, by allowing the play to develop, South can analyze the inferences from the discards, as well as from West's technique. This is far better strategy than the immediate play of the ♢7.

## THE SHAFT (I)

The next two hands illustrate situations that do occur at the table. Occasionally, a player will do his best and still become a victim of an opponent's inept play. Or he may be hurt by an unlucky lie of the cards. Lastly, an opponent's brilliant technique can produce the same results.

---

★This is a very good strategy, and well worth remembering. It is particularly useful when you hold the ♠Q and a three-card club suit containing the Ace or King. By holding the high card for the first round, you are able to clear or strip the suit after you gain the lead.

In our next deal, "poor" South found out what the "strip and stuff" maneuver was all about.

The pass is worth a quick observation. West's pass of the ♡K J was a bit greedy, but I suppose he could take liberties with the guarded ♠Q. South's pass of the ♡Q 9 8 was quite correct. Finally, North had a tough decision, but chose to pass the ♡5. Note that his heart suit headed by the ♡10 was a potential stopper for a slam attempt (prior to the pass).

South seemed to be safe; he had controls in the club and diamond suits, and his hearts, though high, posed no immediate threat since he held a doubleton and had potential discarding opportunities via the spade suit.

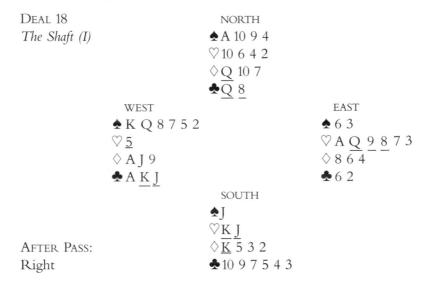

| DEAL 18 | NORTH |
| --- | --- |
| *The Shaft (I)* | ♠A 10 9 4 |
| | ♡10 6 4 2 |
| | ◇Q 10 7 |
| | ♣Q 8 |

| WEST | EAST |
| --- | --- |
| ♠K Q 8 7 5 2 | ♠6 3 |
| ♡5 | ♡A Q 9 8 7 3 |
| ◇A J 9 | ◇8 6 4 |
| ♣A K J | ♣6 2 |

| | SOUTH |
| --- | --- |
| | ♠J |
| | ♡K J |
| AFTER PASS: | ◇K 5 3 2 |
| Right | ♣10 9 7 5 4 3 |

West played the ♣A on trick one (North played his eight, saving the Queen) and immediately shifted to the ◇9. South hesitated before playing the ◇K, as he noted North's discard of the ◇Q. South played the ♠J, which West allowed to hold, North ducked with the ♠10.

South exited with his ♣3, which West grabbed with the King, North dumping the Queen. Now West pushed the ♣J. This drew the ♠A (North), the ♡Q (East), the ♣9, and a slight wince from South. Now the ◇A J fetched the remaining diamonds from North and East, and established South's ◇2 as a thirteener. South's wince became a genuine expression of pain as West now played the ♡5.

The ♡K won the trick (only a rank novice in the East seat would take the Ace). Realizing the futility of either minor suit, South desperately hoped to find the ♡A doubleton. But his ♡J found the ♠Q instead, and he claimed for the balance.★

You might feel a bit sorry for South, but the real tears should be reserved for West in the next hand.

## THE SHAFT (II)

This has to be one of the most amazing deals ever played. The score toward a 100-point game was West 86, North 99, East 98, and South 85. West was dealt a freak and he passed the ◇Q J 9 to North. South, contemplating slam, passed the ♡3 2 and ◇2. South reasoned that with so many high cards and spade blockage, ♠A K J 10, his doom would be to eat the ♠Q. Since scores were close, that player who ate the ♠Q would probably lose unless South and West each took thirteen points. East passed his ♣A K J to South, and slam looked more inviting. West could not believe his six-high yarborough.† Yet he was destined to lose the game against *no* slam! Watch South do his thing.

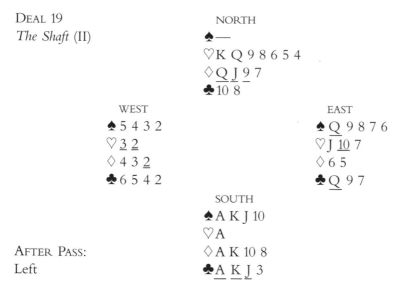

DEAL 19
*The Shaft* (II)

NORTH
♠ —
♡ K Q 9 8 6 5 4
◇ Q J 9 7
♣ 10 8

WEST
♠ 5 4 3 2
♡ 3 2
◇ 4 3 2
♣ 6 5 4 2

EAST
♠ Q 9 8 7 6
♡ J 10 7
◇ 6 5
♣ Q 9 7

SOUTH
♠ A K J 10
♡ A
◇ A K 10 8
♣ A K J 3

AFTER PASS:
Left

The ♣2 went to the ten, Queen, and Ace. South longed to set up diamonds, but feared that a bad break might let an opponent pick up a

★This result is comparable to that of a "fix" in bridge. The bad result is beyond your control.
†A term from bridge and whist, meaning a nine-high or lower hand.

heart discard to rook South's slam try. In the early game, with low scores, this might be sound, since there would be time to recover from a bad score. Instead South decided to psych (i.e., bluff) a slam try. West would think so because of the low pass cards he received, and East might, too, because he failed to pass a low heart. So South led his ♠A with authority. East, fearing slam, held up his well-guarded Queen of spades, and North shed his ♣8. Next South led his ♠K, North shed a high diamond, and East again held up his ♠Q. East mumbled how he wished that he had passed a low heart to South. South cashed his ♠J 10 and East was *forced* to lay off. North discarded two more diamonds. When South cashed his ♣K J, leaving West with the ♣4 and South with the ♣3, North ditched his ♡Q 9. South was correct to play on clubs instead of on diamonds, lest he lose his ♣3 in the end. Note that only *two* club tricks should be cashed, lest West win the fourth round with his four and bury South alive by a heart return. If clubs had split 4-3-3-3, South could have gone slam, but he saw a different club shape on the third round. Besides, East was still transfixed by the fact that South was shooting. South ran his diamonds, Ace-King first, West followed low, and North shed more hearts. East threw a heart on the third diamond lead. East should have realized that his ♠Q would not have mattered, that dumping her on South would have been right, but then we would have no story. Perhaps East wanted to punish the player who stopped slam by making him eat the Queen. I personally do not recommend this tactic, for it may earn you the animosity of your fellow players. If the ♠Q has no value in stopping a slam, dump her. South now cashed his ♡A.

To trick twelve South led a fourth diamond, squeezing West.* If he had cast the ♣4, South's ♣3 would have won the Moonshot. If West had kept his ♣4, he would have stopped slam, but West's eating the ♠Q here would hardly have been worth the bother to him. West forlornly hoped that East would dump the ♠Q on South's last diamond, thus saving the game for West, but no chance. East was still in a trance. East *stayed* in a trance. West threw his ♡2, and East saved his ♠Q for the last trick. And the lowly ♣4 gobbled up North's last heart and East's infamous ♠Q. So West absorbed 14 points and South 12, ending the scores at West 100, North 99, East 98, and South 97. I wonder how many players could have predicted that West with his hand would eat 14 points?

---

*A somewhat unusual situation, created by the inept play of the East player.

**MORAL:** If the spade suit is not critical during a slam try and you hold the ♠Q, let her go at your first opportunity.

Psychology is important in Hearts. Learning card-play technique is important, but this alone will not win in the long run. You must also learn how to play your *opponents*.

## THE SODERLUND SQUEEZE VARIETY I

The "squeeze" play is a term taken from Bridge, and occurs when a player is forced to protect two (or more) suits at one time. In Bridge, there is a "dummy" hand, and the expert declarer (person playing the hand) can execute this maneuver quite easily. In Hearts, the true squeeze play is very rare, as the opponents' hands are concealed, and the player often has to guess the lie of the cards. We occasionally see the squeeze in the Jack of Diamonds variation; in the regular game, it can occur only when a player is attempting to Shoot the Moon. I have

### Soderlund Squeeze
### Variety One— 3/98

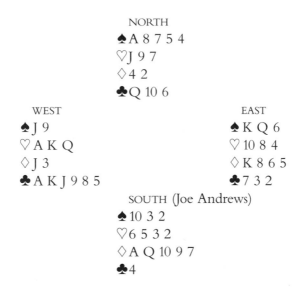

NORTH
♠A 8 7 5 4
♡J 9 7
◇4 2
♣Q 10 6

WEST
♠J 9
♡A K Q
◇J 3
♣A K J 9 8 5

EAST
♠K Q 6
♡10 8 4
◇K 8 6 5
♣7 3 2

SOUTH (Joe Andrews)
♠10 3 2
♡6 5 3 2
◇A Q 10 9 7
♣4

seen some bizarre variations created by poor discarding. The play was named for the late Jack Soderlund of Tewksbury, MA, whose famous hand from the 1978 National Championship appears later in this book.

The amazing hand below was played in a Zone game in March of 1998. It illustrates the most "common" variety of the squeeze. It is still a "rare bird" however! I am quite familiar with the hand, as the play was executed against me!

It had been a good game, and I was in first place by eighteen points. Two players were in the low nineties, and my closest rival (with a score of eighty-one) knew he was in trouble. It was the dreaded "keeper" hand; however, after the deal, I liked my prospects. The diamonds were a concern, but there were discarding opportunities via the club suit. The hearts were solid, and the spades were safe.

The opening deuce of clubs lead went to the Jack and Queen. The spade eight shift was followed by the 6, 10, and Jack. West pushed the diamond three, and I grabbed East's King with my Ace. I now led a small spade, drawing the Jack and King, as North (obviously) ducked. East, with a hanging spade Queen, led the seven of clubs, and I discarded the diamond ten, as West inserted the Ace.

Fearing a heart discard on his diamond Jack, West played his King of clubs, and I unloaded the nine of diamonds. Had West now tried his lone diamond, I would have grabbed the Queen, and pushed out the spade Queen. But then we would have no story. However, West cashed another club, and North dumped a high heart. East chortled as he dumped his "hot" Queen of spades, while commenting, "nice counting"! But West was in command and cashed the A K Q of hearts, and then grabbed another high club. I saved the diamond Queen, and the last heart, leaving this position.

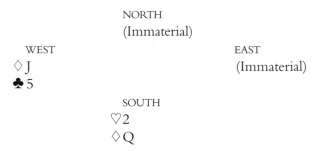

NORTH
(Immaterial)

WEST
◇ J
♣ 5

EAST
(Immaterial)

SOUTH
♡ 2
◇ Q

The club lead was devastating! If I discarded the last heart, West would have had his Moonshot on the spot! Thus, I heaved my diamond lady. NOW, the established Jack of diamonds "squeezed out" my last heart! What a way to end and win a game! The only consolation was that I now had another specimen of the Soderlund Squeeze for my collection!

# Chapter Eight
# HEARTS VARIATIONS

## PARTNERSHIP HEARTS, OR DOUBLES

### Introduction

A most enjoyable and challenging variant of Hearts is the pairs or partnership game called "doubles.\*" The partners must cooperate well to win. Points accumulated by you or your partner are mostly black, charged against your side as a unit. But if you or your partner makes slam, your side wins *white points*. The basic rules of partnership Hearts are the same as those of singles, but strategy differs. Unless trying for slam, you must try to capture at least one heart, hopefully no more. If you and your partner each score zero, opponents score slam and your score is in big trouble, absorbing twenty-six black points. So make every effort to stop slam with *minimal damage*. One way to decrease slams against you is to pass at least one low heart to an opponent on every deal. Rarely will this low-heart pass fail, as below:

|  WEST | EAST |
|-------|------|
| ♠ A J | ♠ K Q 10 2 |
| ♡ K J 10 9 | ♡ Q 8 7 |
| ◇ A K Q J | ◇ — |
| ♣ A | ♣ K Q J 8 4 2 |

*You and your partner play together as a team, and the scoresheet is marked "We" and "They." The pass direction remain the same, *including* the pass *across*.

In a singles game West would probably get stuck with at least twenty points on account of the block in all suits. It looks as if East-West cannot try for a slam because each opponent holds hearts. When East-West misses the ♡A, the situation would seem to be a killer. But in partnership play miracles can happen. West wins the ♣2 lead with his Ace, and cashes three top diamonds, while East dumps three hearts. A fourth diamond lead lets East chuck his ♣2. Next West leads his ♠A, then his ♠J to East's King, and East claims. For you diehards, it is true that if North or South holds ♣10 x x x x, he can stop East's slam. Yet how often will a 5-1 or 6-0 club split occur? Less than ten percent of the time, we believe.* In the rare deal above, East-West would normally have been doomed in hearts. But yes, Virginia, there is a Santa Claus. Always pass a low heart.

The across pass to your partner is one of the most critical judgments in this format. You certainly do not want to hurt your partner with a poor pass or trade the same suit with each other. Expert players use "conventions," which are prearranged agreements for their across passes. Both pairs are urged to develop a convention system to cover this passing situation. Here are a few of the systems used in high level games. By the way, there is no "keep" hand in the Standard Partners Game: thus, you will be facing the across pass decision every third deal.

(1) One partner always passes spades; the other always passes hearts. (This can create a problem with certain spade holdings.)
(2) One partner always passes clubs, the other always passes spades. A twist on this is the exchange of the diamond and spade suits.
(3) One partner agrees never to pass hearts, but leaves an option for the other three suits, while the other partner passes hearts only.

I see potential problems with any system and my opinion is that you should use common sense. For example, if you have a dangerous spade holding (A x, K x x, Q x, etc.), by all means, send the entire suit across the table, unless you have a specific agreement to always pass hearts! This is why the across pass is so challenging and, at times, a matter of guesswork. As you play with a regular partner, you will gradually learn his/her passing tendencies and patterns.

---

*In Hearts, the percentages are difficult to calculate, because suit distributions are greatly affected by the pass.

## The High-Low, or Echo

One key convention for pairs play is the high-low signal from bridge, modified somewhat for Hearts. If you hold exactly two clubs or diamonds, play the higher card first, except that you must play the ♣2 from ♣x 2 on the forced opening lead. For example:

| YOU | PARTNER |
|---|---|
| ♠ Q 10 4 2 | ♠ J 7 6 |
| ♣ 10 6 | ♣ A K 3 |

Partner wins the ♣2 opening lead with his King, then cashes his Ace. You throw your ten, next your six. This is your "echo," the high-low signal to tell your partner that you now have no club left. Partner leads his ♣3 and you discard your ♠Q.

When you hold ♣10 9 3, first play the nine, then later the ten. This low-high order signals *more* than two club cards in hand. Partner might shift to diamonds, realizing that clubs are futile. This can be doubly important if your side lacks the ♠Q. If partner holds three or four cards of a suit and you signal low-high to show at least three cards yourself, another lead of this suit would be dangerous.

| YOU | PARTNER |
|---|---|
| ♠ K 8 7 3 | ♠ Q J 10 4 2 |
| ♡ 6 4 3 | ♡ 10 2 |
| ♢ 10 6 4 3 | ♢ A K Q 2 |
| ♣ 8 7 | ♣ A 4 |

Let us first see what might happen in this situation when the high-low echo is not used. Partner wins the ♣2 opening lead with his Ace and runs diamonds, hoping that you hold two or fewer for your side. So he cashes his ♢Q for round three and you follow. Now he probably exits via his ♣4, saving his ♢2. Your opponents, with nine solid clubs and hearts between them, get on lead. If either is long in clubs, he runs them, while his partner discards hearts. If you jettison your ♠Q early, a slam scores against you; if you do not, the slam may be made anyway. Much depends on the actual holdings, but why go through this anguish?

Let us replay the deal and use the high-low signal. First, the ♣A wins and you throw your eightspot. Partner cashes his ♢A and you play your six. Next he cashes his ♢K, and you play your ten to show partner at least three diamonds. Also, this tells him that leading the ♢Q

is useless and that it may set up the Jack if an opponent happens to hold
◇J x x x. So your partner shifts to his club and you play your ♣7. If
alert, partner will remember your *eightspot* on the first club lead, mark-
ing you with only two clubs. This reveals to him the great club length
and short diamonds of the enemy. These data still may not help to stop
a slam, but the defense will have a better chance if it has an idea how
key cards lie.

In another deal, you hold two diamonds and four clubs. When your
partner cashes his ◇A, you play high first, then low later. This echo
tells him that you are now void. He can cash his ◇K to let you discard
a heart to stop a possible enemy slam. He can save his ◇2 for a later
exit and play his last club now. With right play and normal lie of the
cards, your side should escape with only *one* black point.

The high-low signal is also useful for reading the lie of suits,
particularly for slam. For example:

| YOU | PARTNER |
|---|---|
| ♠8 4 2 | ♠ A K Q J 5 |
| ♡6 4 | ♡ A K 10 8 5 2 |
| ◇A J 4 2 | ◇ K |
| ♣J 7 6 5 | ♣ A |

Your side is playing high-low. Partner, with slam in mind, wins the ♣2
opening with his Ace, and leads his dry ◇K to void his diamonds. The
King happens to win, for you have the Ace. But if an opponent held
the ◇A, he would most likely have won and returned a spade. In the
present case, partner leads his ♠5, which an opponent wins. On a spade
return, partner plays his Ace and then his King, drawing your last
spade. You play your four of spades first, then your eightspot—to show
you hold more than two spades—and finally your deuce.

By the rule of high-low, in the minor suits we echo with any two
cards; in the spade and heart suits, however, we use only the Jack and
lower cards. For example, if you hold ♠K 2, you would not lead the
King to begin a signal. In hearts you should keep honor cards (ten and
higher) until you get some sort of count on the hands. Also, hearts are
usually not led until the middle or endgame. If you hold only low to
middle cards, Jack down, you can signal high-low. If you hold the ♣2
after the pass, your forced ♣2 lead cannot be a signal.

In the deal above, your partner has drawn your last spade. Now he
cashes his ♠J and you cast the ♡6, breaking the suit. Next your part-

ner cashes his ♡A and you play your ♡4, completing your high-low echo in one suit on leads of two suits. With ♡9 6 4 you would have instead played the six first, next the nine on the ♡A. But in the case above your partner learns that you began life with only two hearts. So partner reads eight hearts on your side, and these leave ♡Q J 9 7 3 with opponents. If enemy hearts fall 5-0 or 4-1 or split 3-2 normally, and the heart pictures do not drop doubleton, right defense will stop your slam. Therefore, partner should quit a slam quest and go normally for low score. After cashing his ♡A he should lead his ♡10. If both opponents duck, next he leads his ♡K. By now he should have a complete count on hearts, and he would play to slam or exit via his ♡2. Probably an opponent will take the ♡10. Partner now escapes from the hand with minimum damage via his escape card, his ♡2. If he lacked the ♡2, but had, say, ♡A K 10 9 7 6, the best line is to play to drop the ♡Q J dry by cashing his ♡A K. If hearts split 3-2, he escapes on the third round, having stripped opponents' hearts. Thanks to your helpful high-low, he was able to get a count and to play accordingly.

## Unblocking

Assume that you hold three hearts without any of the pictures. (With the ♡Q in your hand, partner's slam is almost sure; if you hold the ♡J, partner still has good chances.) Let me illustrate:

|  YOU  |  PARTNER  |
|-------|-----------|
| ♡7 6 3 | ♡ A K 10 8 5 2 |

The play is as above. Partner runs spades and you cast the ♡6. Next he cashes his ♡A and you play the seven, advertising *at least three* hearts. If hearts split 2-2, they fall for slam; if hearts split 3-1 normally, one opponent will be forced to score his honor on the third round, and your partner will be safe from further heart leads. If the suit splits 4-0, partner will lead his ♡A K 10, in this order. That opponent who scores his ♡J or ♡Q will have left one heart *higher than the two*.

In pair games an essential feature is to locate the ♠Q early. There are a few ways to show your partner where the ♠Q lies:

(1) If you lead a spade early, you deny that you hold the ♠Q.
(2) A high-low signal in clubs may be used to show the ♠Q in hand. A more refined convention is to play an *even* club on trick one, apart from the forced ♣2 opening, to show the ♠Q, and an *odd* club to deny

it.* Both the King and Jack of clubs are *odd,* the Ace and Queen *even.* If one holds the ♠Q but no club, signal in diamonds. These *odd* and *even* signals are good, but they will backfire occasionally for lack of a right club.

(3) A high-low signal in spades may be used to show the Queen.

## Communication by Inference; Cooperation; Clearance

*Sometimes a hand looks hopeless,* but once in a while an ingenious pair can turn the tables with a little luck and hard work. North, with losers galore, and South, with the ♠Q poorly guarded, cooperate beautifully in Deal 20 to make a slam.

Game was close and hinged on this deal. Fearing slam, East had passed the ♠Q and two low hearts to South. West had passed the ◊J and two low hearts to North. To him, slam seemed out of the question. Hearts and clubs were well stopped. East snapped up the ♣2 opening lead with his Ace and led the ♠5. East knew that his partner lacked the ♠Q. North stopped the smokeout momentarily with his ♠A and returned his dry ◊J. This West grabbed with his Ace, and led the ♠10, dropping South's Queen. South paused to consider. Since his side had eaten the ♠Q, a slam was his only chance to escape the heavy loss. If the ♡A lay North, South had hope. South led his ♡K, which won.

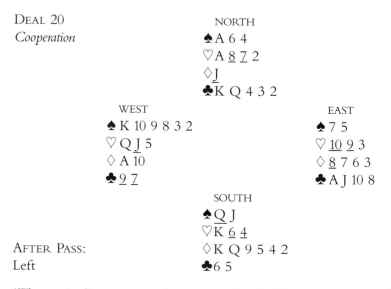

DEAL 20
*Cooperation*

　　　　　　　　　NORTH
　　　　　　　　　♠A 6 4
　　　　　　　　　♡A <u>8 7</u> 2
　　　　　　　　　◊<u>J</u>
　　　　　　　　　♣K Q 4 3 2

　　WEST　　　　　　　　　　　　EAST
　♠K 10 9 8 3 2　　　　　　　♠7 5
　♡Q J 5　　　　　　　　　　♡<u>10</u> 9 3
　◊A 10　　　　　　　　　　◊<u>8</u> 7 6 3
　♣<u>9 7</u>　　　　　　　　　　♣A J 10 8

　　　　　　　　　SOUTH
　　　　　　　　　♠<u>Q</u> J
　　　　　　　　　♡K <u>6</u> 4
AFTER PASS:　　　◊K Q 9 5 4 2
Left　　　　　　　♣6 5

*Whatever signaling system you and your partner select should be *committed to memory*. Otherwise, the problems will be most unpleasant.

South, realizing he had nothing to lose and remembering that the ♣K had not appeared, won five diamond tricks, King-Queen first. West tossed three low spades and his last club; East shed his last two hearts, correctly assuming that his partner guarded hearts. North carefully discarded his ♣4 3, his low spade, and his two low hearts, leaving:

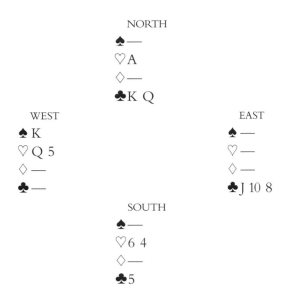

NORTH
♠ —
♡ A
♢ —
♣ K Q

WEST
♠ K
♡ Q 5
♢ —
♣ —

EAST
♠ —
♡ —
♢ —
♣ J 10 8

SOUTH
♠ —
♡ 6 4
♢ —
♣ 5

South led his ♡6 and North claimed slam. South was lucky to find his partner with the ♡A and two top clubs. Note that this line of play is the only way to salvage the deal. If South runs diamonds before cashing his ♡K, North must guess whether to bare his ♡A and keep the ♣K Q 4, or to keep the ♡A 8. North would probably keep the extra club and East would come to a club trick to kill the slam. Finally, if South keeps clubs after eating the ♠Q, North gets on lead too early and must guess who holds the ♡K, with plenty of chances to go wrong. Laying down the ♡K early to reveal its location is the clearest and easiest way for partners to communicate.

In doubles play *capturing the first heart is vital.* This relieves your side of an enemy slam threat, while keeping your own slam chances open, or enables you to exit cleanly. There are exceptions. If you lack the ♠Q, it may be dangerous to win the first heart lead. You hold:

♠J 10 3    ♡A 5 2    ♢A K Q J 4 2    ♣10

It would be foolish to run diamonds unless you know for sure that partner holds the ♠Q. Otherwise, the player with the ♠Q could be short of diamonds, and your diamond-run effort might cost you fifteen points—expensive slam insurance. Say you hold:

♠J 10 4 2   ♡9 8 7 3   ◇Q 7 4   ♣A K

You win the opening ♣2 with your Ace, while partner sheds a diamond. The ♣K next is a sound play, for it lets partner shed a heart at once. Only a wild club split begets the ♠Q. Now you can exit safely in diamonds or spades. If partner has a slam hand, he can take control. If he has a low-card hand, your side may escape for five or fewer points. Note that the exit must be in spades or diamonds. A heart exit may find partner void or missing the Ace, and it could disrupt slam.

A convenient thing about discarding is that it lets you unload useless or dangerous high cards on your partner's winners. For example, see Deal 21.

West has passed the ♡K 9 and ♣K. South had passed his two low hearts and the ♠A, praying that the ♠Q would not land in his hand. Although relieved about this, he was depressed when he picked up the ♡J 6. To West, everything was beautiful! His ♠Q was well guarded, he held the key top heart and two deuces, plus that trusty old ♣3. North and South looked doomed. The red suits were bad, clubs very bad, and North-South had no prospect of smoking out the ♠Q. North's ♣K

DEAL 21
*Clearance*

| | NORTH | |
|---|---|---|
| | ♠J 10 2 | |
| | ♡K 9 7 | |
| | ◇K Q J 7 3 | |
| | ♣K J | |

| WEST | | EAST |
|---|---|---|
| ♠A Q 8 6 5 3 | | ♠K 7 |
| ♡A 5 2 | | ♡Q 10 8 4 3 |
| ◇A 2 | | ◇10 6 5 |
| ♣9 3 | | ♣8 6 4 |

| | SOUTH | |
|---|---|---|
| | ♠9 4 | |
| | ♡J 6 | |
| | ◇9 8 4 | |
| | ♣A Q 10 7 5 2 | |

AFTER PASS:
Left

won trick one and North led his ◇J in order to drive out the Ace. West snapped this up with dispatch, and led his ◇2 to void his diamonds. North won with his ◇Q and shifted to his ♠J, which East-West ducked. North led his ♠2, and, when East rose with the King, North was very grateful that his partner lacked it. East led his ♣4 to South's Ace. When the Jack fell from North, South led his ♣Q. West chuckled as he tossed his ♠Q, but winced when North shed his ♠10, a brilliant discard. South won three more club tricks and North dumped all three of his hearts. South led the ◇9, and North's ◇K 7 3 took the balance.

## The Vienna Coup

Next we offer an extraordinary, unbelievable, and fantastic deal from a state-championship tournament. The pair that won this slam was accused of cheating, of being covered with horseshoes (i.e., of being unusually lucky), and of using marked cards, but none of this was the case. Deal 22 helped to win a game.

James Clay, top whist authority of his time, first published the Vienna Coup as a double-dummy problem, probably in his *Treatise on Whist* in 1864. Clay described it as "The great Vienna Coup." The coup is a true squeeze prepared by deliberately cashing a winner to establish an enemy master card of its suit as a vital threat in the end position.

The opening ♣2 lead went to the King, Jack, and six. South led his ◇10 to seven, King, and Jack. North next cashed the ♣Q, taking West's

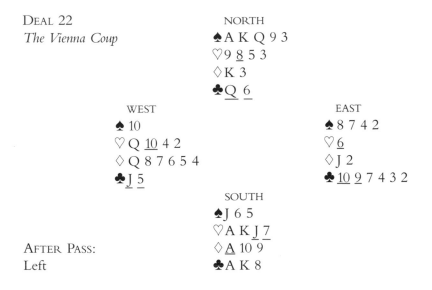

DEAL 22
*The Vienna Coup*

NORTH
♠A K Q 9 3
♡9 8 5 3
◇K 3
♣Q 6

WEST
♠ 10
♡Q 10 4 2
◇Q 8 7 6 5 4
♣J 5

EAST
♠8 7 4 2
♡6
◇J 2
♣10 9 7 4 3 2

SOUTH
♠J 6 5
♡A K J 7
◇A 10 9
♣A K 8

AFTER PASS:
Left

five. North led his ♠9 to South's Jack. The ♣A won, West shed the ◇6, and North shed a low heart. South now suspected West's shape, and he led the ♠6. West heaved the ♡10, still leaving the ♡Q guarded, but hoped that East might hold a high spade honor. But North stepped up with his ♠A and made the highly imaginative play of a low heart. South cashed the ♡A K, establishing that West held the Queen, seemingly to doom slam. Next South led his last spade. North, sensing the position, won with his King and played his Queen. East's hand was now dead. South ditched the ♡7, and West kept his ◇Q 8 and ♡Q dry, as shown in the matrix.

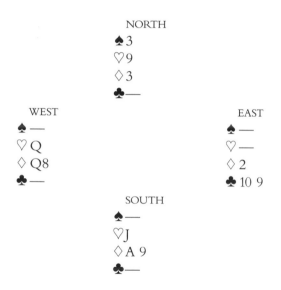

NORTH
♠ 3
♡ 9
◇ 3
♣ —

WEST
♠ —
♡ Q
◇ Q8
♣ —

EAST
♠ —
♡ —
◇ 2
♣ 10 9

SOUTH
♠ —
♡ J
◇ A 9
♣ —

North led his last spade, South shed the ♡J and West was sunk. If West were to shed a diamond, South's ◇A 9 would win the last two tricks, or else North's ♡9 would complete the twenty-six points for slam. Though rare in bridge despite the dummy hand, the Vienna Coup in Hearts is unique—a work of art! Luck, plus South's intellect and North's imagination, proved unbeatable in this deal of a lifetime.

The Zone features a rather intriguing form of Partnership Hearts, which is truly a "hybrid" version of the standard game. This is attributable to the fact that there is not (as of this revision) a format for the standard game. Some very ingenious zoners developed this variation, which is very clever and highly challenging. Here is a brief summary of the rules for the variety II game:

(1) The game limit is 100 points, and each player retains an individual score (instead of the combined "we/they" in the standard format.) The game ends when any player reaches 100 points. The scores are then added and the side with the lowest COMBINED total is declared the winner. Thus, if WE have 45 and 65 points, and THEY have 100 and 30 points (respectively), WE win, as our combined total is 110 to their 130 points. This is rather interesting, as one of their players has the low score! Some games are decided by a mere handful of points!

(2) There is a "keeper" or hold hand, which means that the pass is eliminated for this one hand. It is imperative that you "dump" the spade Queen on the opponents as soon as possible. (There will be a rare occasion when it is necessary to take the Queen to stop a Moon.)

(3) Shooting the Moon is very tricky in this version, and you must do it alone, as in the individual game. Your partner can make some key discards to set up your hand; however, he/she cannot take any points while you are "shooting." If your side splits the twenty-six points in any fashion, you are stuck with twenty-six points. This is the one significant difference from the standard game. If you do shoot, you add twenty-six points to everyone (including your partner)! However, the opponents are taking fifty-two points; thus, you still gain twenty-six points for the hand.

(4) Passing strategy for the across pass is very easy. You may still use any convention you wish. One very clever system was devised by two Zone experts, Lady Lauren and Tybee Dave. On their across pass, they note each other's scores. Whoever has the higher score (of the partnership at that time), always passes hearts (including the deuce or lowest card in the suit), and the person with the lower score always passes spades. Of course, there are exceptions, and one must be flexible. For example, if the partner scheduled to pass spades has the Queen and five or more "backers," the plan shifts. Now the strategy is to pass the diamond suit with the deuce or club suit with the three. This alerts the partner to lead the control (low) card as soon as possible, thus clearing the path for the unloading of the spade Queen! The key is the partnership understanding. "Lauren" and "Dave" have perfected their partnership game to a level that makes them almost unbeatable! Spades is another game where a fine-tuned partnership can be very formidable.

Basically, that's it. It is a fine game, with lots of nuances. It does take some adjusting. Awareness of the score is essential. It is a good idea to post the score, and differential, in order to keep your partner on his/her toes! There are times when it is perfectly correct to throw the spade Queen on your partner—in order to end the game and still have the lowest combined score. Otherwise, the strategy and technique of the standard game still applies. Try the variety II game—you will like it!

The tournament organizer of the Eclectic Site for the Zone has written a very detailed and useful guideline for this partnership game. Laurie (of Montreal, Canada) is a very brilliant player who has become especially proficient in this variety II format. Here are some of her stratagems.

## PARTNERSHIP HEARTS—VARIETY II STRATEGY AND TECHNIQUE (Contributed by "ECLECTIC")

### Note—"Pard" means "Partner"

*The pard pass is what makes or breaks the game, as it is the sole hand that gives the advantage for you or your partner to Moon. Therefore, those three cards are critical. One partner should pass their three highest spades. While the other should pass any three cards that either help them to Moon (i.e., short suit themselves or dump low hearts). If the non-spades passer cannot Moon, they should pass whichever their highest cards might be. Certainly an A of hearts can be useful, but not a K or Q of hearts (without the Ace) as they could simply mean four points and do not ensure control. In a hand where AKQJ10 of diamonds are present, passing the AKQ ensures control of that suit. For the spades passer the pass is a simple one. However, for the other person there is more thought required.*

*To ensure that you take advantage of every opportunity, there exists an added twist (this one few use). When scores are tied (i.e., first hand 0-0) one person is designated as the spades passer. Then, throughout the game it is the high scoring person who should receive spades. This is done as a protective cushion. In the event that the high person possesses the Q of spades, they will have three additional spades as back-up. Or if a Moon is somehow lost in the first hands (i.e., hearts are broken) then the high person does not run the risk of eating the Q of spades since they can flog it out.*

### Non-Pard Passing

*Clearly the first priority is to indicate to your partner if you have the Q of spades. Voiding clubs is an excellent way to do this. On the first hand, you can* toss out an unwanted K or A of spades if passed to you. Also, it is good practice to take the first club trick and lead back with a spade. Only one run of spades, however, then you wait for your partner to also lead a spade. If they do not you assume they have the A, K spades or Q, in which case you can come back high to locate their short suit and maintain control of the play so that spades aren't flogged.

## Common Mistakes:

Solo playing has to be the worst type of partnership playing. One should always think in twos!! It is not enough for me to get through a round with zero points if my partner eats twenty!! In many hands that I've viewed, there was usually a way out. If, for instance, I have K, 10, 2, 3 of diamonds I don't play the K on an A, I play the 10. The K stays back to regain control of the play when needed. That's the key issue here. Never allow the opps to control the lead and never allow your partner to get boxed into a long suit with no hope of an out.

Another solo strategy is to take the trick high and comeback low, ensuring that someone else eats the Q. Can't do that with pards. Since no team member is going to drop the Q unless they are certain their partner is void in that suit. A few make assumptions for fear of eating it, but that is not considered to be good pard playing and that team will not last very long together.

There is little point to keeping spades in your hand if you know that your pard has the Q. The only spades you should keep are boss spades, which should be used to divert the play.

Rarely should you drop a heart on the opps. Always try to drop the first heart on your pard, give them the option to Moon if they can, but never give the opps the same opportunity. Drop a troublesome card before a heart when unsure. Once your pard drops a heart, it is a good practice to comeback low in that suit, as now you've given your pard the option of dumping a Q of spades safely or allowing your pard to dump high problematic hearts to the opps.

Watch your pard's discards and count all suits. Most good players only count the suits necessary to play their hands. However, in pard Hearts you need to be able to count twice. Once for your hand and a second time for your pard's. If on an A of clubs lead, your pard plays a 4 then later plays the K. One of two things is present: 1) they have the Q and need control or 2) they want to Moon or suspect the opps might. As in spades, it is good practice to lead back with what your partner led. Get back into their hand if they are dumping low and taking high. Always remember your pard's highest card before leading low.

Equally, forgetting that two people are essentially Mooning rather than one.

*Most non-pard passes are high clubs or diamonds, seldom a heart. This is rather silly, since at the first opportunity the opps pard can dump all high hearts, thereby dramatically improving their Moon chances. My favorite pass is: A2 clubs and 10 of hearts. I would do this with AK872 of clubs and only if I had a heart greater than 10.*

*Another common mistake is not eating the Q on your partners behalf. This is a tough one for most solo Hearts players. Those used to "only one advance" type games will be quick to do so. But not the "two advance" type players. Many factors play into the equation here. Score counting (combining your and your partner's scores and then opps) each hand is essential. If you're down in combined points and you know your partner has the Q, eat it if their score is twenty or more points above yours. The idea being to lessen the chances that one of you will bust the game to lose.*

*I've even seen some games where an opp deliberately eats a Q of spades with no Moon chances. Why? Simply to end the game because they were leading in combined points (Opps: 89/23 Us: 65/72 or 112/139. With a twenty-seven point lead they can safely eat the Q of spades and a few hearts while still winning the game). Not a particularly joyous event, but none the less effective. What a fun game this can be!*

## JACK OF DIAMONDS (PLUS TEN)

As the Hearts game evolved, many modifications were added. Some were cumbersome, such as having the $\heartsuit$Q also count thirteen black points and/or adding a joker to count five. Others proved helpful, such as the pass of cards to opponents and the mandatory $\clubsuit$2 opening lead. In one innovation, the $\diamondsuit$J (or $\diamondsuit$10) as a bonus card always counts ten white points for its captor, regardless of other scoring. Slam scores twenty-six white points, or thirty-six points if the player also took the $\diamondsuit$J.

The Jack of Diamonds variation (often called "Omnibus") is regaining popularity. It was introduced in the late 1920s, and reached its peak in the early 1960s. It does add a significance to the diamond suit, and requires a high level of concentration. The only drawback to playing with the diamond Jack is that it does lengthen the game; this can be offset by agreeing to a fifty or seventy-five point limit. Here are some helpful strategy guidelines.

Scoring the $\diamondsuit$J alters strategy. The four ways to capture the $\diamondsuit$J are:

(1) By leading it to win after it has become a master card.

(2) By dropping it unguarded on straight leads of higher diamonds. For example, you run your ◇A K Q from ◇A K Q x x x, hoping that the Jack, with two or fewer guards, will fall.

(3) By scoring it fourth hand (led up to) after other players with higher cards have ducked; or by playing it on partner's tricks in doubles.

(4) By passing all your diamonds, then picking up the ◇J by winning all the last few tricks in the endgame. Let us detail all these below:

## Jack Becomes Master

The ♠Q and most hearts have been played, and slam is not possible. You lead your ♡9 to your opponent's Queen, which wins. Your opponent cashes his ◇A K Q, trying to drop the ◇J, but fails. Later, a club to your Ace lets you in to score your established (master) ◇J, and you win ten white points.

| YOU | OPPONENT |
|---|---|
| ♠ — | ♠ — |
| ♡ 9 | ♡ Q |
| ◇ J 10 9 8 | ◇ A K Q 3 2 |
| ♣ A 6 4 | ♣ J 8 |

## Dropping the Jack

| YOU | OPPONENT |
|---|---|
| ♠ — | ♠ — |
| ♡ — | ♡ 10 4 |
| ◇ J 10 9 | ◇ A K Q 3 2 |
| ♣ K Q 9 4 3 | ♣ A |

Let us now look at a situation (see diagram) in which you hold the ◇J with two guards (supporting cards), and your opponent holds the ◇J K Q. You lead any club, and he wins with his Ace. Now he leads the ◇A K Q, and on the third round your ◇J falls. Similarly, a ◇J with only one guard will drop under the doubleton ◇A K holding.

## Diamond Jack Led Up To

Suppose West leads his ◇9 (see diagram). The ◇K and ◇Q have already been played, and North is void. East, the third hand, has the choice of two losing plays: to go up with his Ace in the hope of dropping the Jack dry, or to duck in the hope that his Ace will drop the $\Diamond$J from West on the next round. In the actual layout, this is a guess for East, and South benefits from West's diamond lead. Some foxy players

NORTH

$\Diamond$ —

WEST

$\Diamond$ 9 5

EAST

$\Diamond$ A 3

SOUTH

$\Diamond$ J 7

who hold the $\Diamond$J with several supporting cards (but missing the $\Diamond$A K and/or $\Diamond$Q) will underlead their $\Diamond$J with the hope of coaxing out the high cards. This way, their $\Diamond$J will eventually become established. This strategy will work if you have enough side entry cards to obtain the lead often, and if an opponent does not hold great diamond length. Finally, there is the $\spadesuit$Q to worry about. A $\Diamond$J married to a $\spadesuit$Q may be a pinochle, but it is also worth three losing points in Hearts! Now note another situation with three cards in each hand.

NORTH

$\Diamond$ K 10 9

WEST

$\Diamond$ J 5 3

EAST

$\Diamond$ Q 7 6

SOUTH

$\Diamond$ A 8 2

North leads his big casino (the $\Diamond$10), hoping to entice out the Ace: East ducks and South ponders. He does not want to play his Ace now and fan air, so he ducks also and West scores his $\Diamond$J for free. Usually third hand plays high on the diamond lead lest this happen. South should have played his Ace, for it would have been useless anyway if West held the Jack, as he in fact did. There are exceptions to this third-hand-high rule:

(1) If you know that the $\Diamond$J lies in another hand, save your high honor.

(2) If the player under you plays high, duck, especially on the first lead of the suit.

(3) If you suspect strongly that the ♠Q will alight on your diamond trick, by all means duck. Nothing is more embarrassing than letting an opponent score a free ◇J—except eating the ♠Q on your high diamond!* As always, use your judgment in every position.

## Void in Diamonds: Jack-of-Diamonds Endplay

The endplay is the prettiest way to capture His Nibs, the ◇J. This requires skill and planning by players who can execute the maneuver. I have seen deals where a player will stumble into an ending by accident. Most endplays, however, require hard work and precise timing, as well as luck, as in Deal 23A.

South has passed his ◇J 4 and ♡Q to West. It took intestinal fortitude to keep that ♡K, but South's three spade guards looked safe enough.† The ♣2 went to the Queen and South's Ace; South returned his ♣3, going to East's ♣10. East led his ◇7. South shed his ♡10, confident that his ♠K would not hurt him. West, not knowing where the ◇A was, played his King and then shifted to his ♠J, both of which North ducked. East hemmed and hawed and finessed his Ace with a prayer. When South played his King, East sighed in relief. East's ♠2 then went to South's ten. The ♠9 drew two low spades, and the ♡J from East. Next the spade eightspot drew high hearts from West and East and the ♠Q from North. North realized that he needed that ◇J to offset ten of his ♠Q black points. He suspected that the ◇J lay West

DEAL 23A
*Jack-of-Diamonds*
*Endplay*

NORTH
♠Q 7 5 3
♡K 9 5
◇A 10 3 2
♣7 2

WEST
♠J 6 4
♡Q 4 3
◇K Q J 6 4
♣8 6

EAST
♠A 2
♡J 8 7
◇9 8 7 5
♣Q 10 9 5

*If you hold the ♠Q in a safe hand, and the ◇J has *not* been played, you should save your ♠Q for the player who wins the ◇J. This will help to balance the score.
†In this case, the retention of the ♠K was strategic, since the side suits were safe and the supporting spades high.

SOUTH
♠ K 10 9 8
♡ A <u>10</u> 6 2
◇ —
♣ A K <u>J</u> 4 3

AFTER PASS:
Left

because East had led in diamonds and South was obviously void of them. Reluctant to lead away from his ◇A, North led his ♡9, which South ducked with the ♡6. North still thought that West held the ♡A and continued with the ♡5, drawing the deuce from South and West's

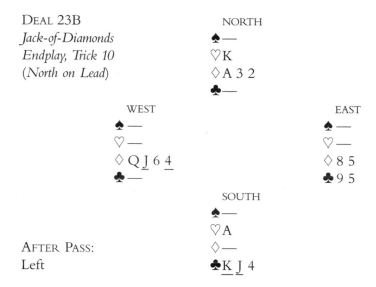

DEAL 23B
*Jack-of-Diamonds*
*Endplay, Trick 10*
*(North on Lead)*

NORTH
♠ —
♡ K
◇ A 3 2
♣ —

WEST
♠ —
♡ —
◇ Q J 6 <u>4</u>
♣ —

EAST
♠ —
♡ —
◇ 8 5
♣ 9 5

SOUTH
♠ —
♡ A
◇ —
♣ K J 4

AFTER PASS:
Left

♣ K <u>J</u> 4

three. (Now see Deal 23B). North remembered that the ♡A was still at large and led his King. South rose with his Ace and claimed, including the ◇J. South absorbed three hearts and the ◇J to net seven white points.

Note how carefully South held up his ♡A until the last moment when he got a count. If West had got on lead in diamonds, however, South would have discarded his high hearts on diamond leads and escaped with a beautiful score: one black point.

This tactic of voiding one's diamonds by passing them is good, sound strategy. All you have to do is keep track of the low cards and count nonheart suits, and you should be in good shape. Of course, if your hand is bad and/or if you eat the ♠Q, you must go all out to grab that ◊J.

## TRIO HEARTS: A CHALLENGE FOR THREE

### Basic Trio

A very fine game of Hearts that allows for a considerable level of skill is three-handed, called "trio Hearts." Dealer serves 17 cards to each player, plus the odd card, which he deals to his LHO, who plays *two* cards, both clubs if possible, on trick one in order to equalize his hand with the others. Except for the pass of *four* cards instead of three, other rules are much the same as for quartet Hearts. Thirteen-card variants are being researched in the hope of finding a good variant that will take no more time per deal to play than quartet in parties and tourneys. Other differences from quartet are strategic, to wit:

### Slams in Trio

Moonshots are generally more difficult to make because distributions tend to be more erratic. After the pass a suit of seven or eight cards is common. Usually a slam scores if a defender errs badly or the gofor (slam-minded player) has tops plus great length in one or two suits. A low-heart pass will kill many otherwise makeable slams.

### Spade Guards for the Queen

These are important. Queen fifth or sixth is safe, although Queen fourth is sometimes adequate if headed by Ace or King (i.e., Ace-Queen fifth or King-Queen fifth) to stop enemy spade leads. But with Queen and four low spades you must hope that spades split 5-4-4 or that a spear play is available.

With the Queen and fewer other low spades, pass her. On occasion, you will be dealt Q x x x x. Keep her then, for odds favor an Ace or King pass to you. An opponent with an Ace or King in fewer than five spades is likely to pass it to you. If an opponent holds five spades and you do also, your other opponent will have only three, and a spear play is possible.

## Count and Strip

It is also essential to count suits and to strip enemy hands, as illustrated in typical Deal 24A. West and East appear blessed with safety; that proves to be a mirage. South takes East's ♣2 opening lead with his Ace, and West plays his ♣8 4 on trick one in order to rid himself of the extra card dealt to him.* South shifts to his ◊6, going to East's Ace, and East leads his ♠J, which South and West duck. Next the ♠10 goes to West's Ace, South having ducked; a low-spade return loses to South's nine, and East drops his ♣J. South leads his ◊Q to clear the suit and it wins.

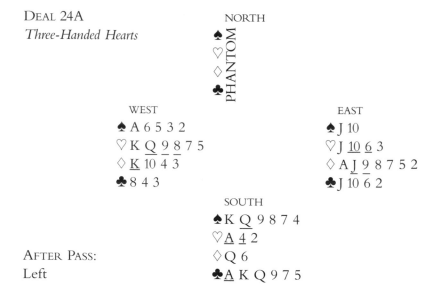

DEAL 24A
*Three-Handed Hearts*

NORTH
♠ ♡ ◊ ♣ PHANTOM

WEST
♠ A 6 5 3 2
♡ K Q 9 8 7 5
◊ K 10 4 3
♣ 8 4 3

EAST
♠ J 10
♡ J 10 6 3
◊ A J 9 8 7 5 2
♣ J 10 6 2

SOUTH
♠ K Q 9 8 7 4
♡ A 4 2
◊ Q 6
♣ A K Q 9 7 5

AFTER PASS:
Left

Now (see Deal 24B) South cashes his ♠K 8, drawing West's last spades and high clubs from East. South then cashes his ♣K, drawing West's three and a high heart from East Had East pitched a diamond, South would have pushed clubs until someone threw a heart. Here, South leads his ♡A, then the ♡4. South is now immune for the rest of the play and escapes with four points.

If hearts split badly, South still survives, for he has the ♡2. This deal

---

*Another variation is to remove the ♣2 from the deck and to make the ♣3 the required opening lead. This allows for an even deal of seventeen cards per player and eliminates the double discard on trick one.

shows how planning the right line of play pays off. In trio Hearts it is only a matter of adjusting.

Another line would be to play the ♡4 instead of the Ace, in hope of a diamond return in order to pitch the ♡A and escape with one point. But if you do this and a heart is returned, take the Ace and exit via the ♡2.

DEAL 24B
*Three-Handed Hearts,*
*Trick 7*

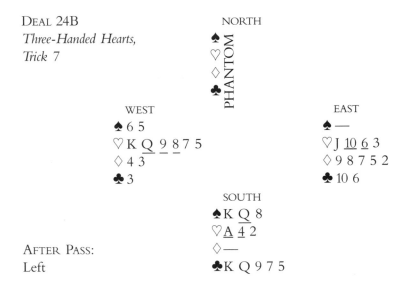

NORTH
♠
♡  PHANTOM
♢
♣

WEST
♠ 6 5
♡ K Q 9 8 7 5
♢ 4 3
♣ 3

EAST
♠ —
♡ J 10 6 3
♢ 9 8 7 5 2
♣ 10 6

SOUTH
♠ K Q 8
♡ A 4 2
♢ —
♣ K Q 9 7 5

AFTER PASS:
Left

## TWO-HANDED HEARTS

### Background and Rules

Hearts lends itself to many variations, and can accommodate from two to seven persons. Although the four-handed variation is best, the three-handed game is quite good and has much of the strategy of the four-handed game.

The real challenge was the development of a good two-handed variation. Hearts has unique features, which made its modification into a "honeymoon whist" type of game very difficult. Then there was the problem of extremes of luck. It seemed that whoever drew the deuces, particularly the deuce of hearts, would have a great advantage. Finally, it was apparent that the standard rules of Hearts would have to be modified for the two-handed game. The solution seemed impossible until my friend, Harriet, came up with a few ingenious suggestions.

Now there is a two-handed game which is highly competitive and exciting. Here is a brief summary of the rules:

(1) A standard deck of fifty-two cards is used.

(2) Remove the four deuces. In the first hand, give the red deuces (hearts and diamonds) to one player, and the black deuces (spades and clubs) to the other player. This arrangement will *alternate* with each hand.

(3) Now deal eleven cards, face down, to each player. The rest of the deck is placed face down and becomes the "stock."

(4) Each player will add the deuces to his hand, thus creating a 13-card holding. Whoever holds the club deuce makes the opening lead, *but* has the right to lead *anything* (That includes a heart, another club besides the deuce, etc.)

(5) The key cards in each hand are the ♠Q, ◊J, and, of course, the heart suit. The same point count applies as in the standard game. The ◊J is worth a bonus of ten white points, to be deducted from your score. It should be rather obvious why low diamond leads can be risky (if you do not hold the Jack). You may allow your opponent to score a free bonus. If you capture all thirteen hearts and the ♠Q, you may deduct twenty-six points from your score *or* add the same to your opponent's score. You do not need the ◊J in order to "shoot the moon."

(6) Whoever wins the opening lead draws a card from the stock. (The loser of the trick then draws, thus restoring his hand to thirteen cards.) You must follow suit whenever possible; otherwise you may discard anything. Thus, your hand is always restored to thirteen cards, until the stock becomes depleted. At that point, each player will now play his hand until both have depleted their holdings. Each trick will consist of two cards, and the winner of the previous trick makes the lead to the next trick.

(7) After the hand is completed, add up the points. If the points are "split," that is, there is no moonshot, the total must always equal sixteen (twenty-six points minus the ten for the Jack). A player may have a negative score if he takes the Jack and less than ten points. A lot of hands will be very close (e.g., 8-8, 10-6, etc.). Then again, the extreme result is a score of minus-9 (the Jack plus one heart) vs. plus-25 for the opponent (the spade Queen and twelve hearts). Moonshots will allow for even wilder variations.

(8) The game ends when one player reaches 100 points. Remember, you must follow suit whenever you can. In this game, there is an honor system, and it is assumed that a player will not renege. Don't forget to alternate the deuces after each hand. Try it—you'll like it!

## Strategy

This is one game where counting is critical. You must learn to keep track of more than one suit at the same time. The deuces are key exit cards and should be saved for the endgame.

If you do not start with the club deuce, you can safely lead clubs early in the hand until your opponent drops this card. If you are dealt the ♠Q with weak support, it is advised that you keep the lead by playing your high cards. You might draw some spade support from the stock.

It is most important that you try to capture a heart trick early in the hand. This removes the threat of a moonshot. If your heart suit consists of high cards (e.g., A K Q, etc.), you might want to avoid a low-heart lead and see if you can draw additional cards in this suit (to set up the possibility of a slam).

Remember, the count in each suit is essential. This particularly applies to spades, especially if your opponent is stranded with the Ace or King and is forced to lead away from this holding.

## THE "DEPRAVATION" PLAY—PART II

There are plays in Hearts which are downright mean and nasty. Although the individuals' game is called "Cutthroat Hearts," there are situations which do draw attention. Earlier, we saw the "Rubin's Maneuver." I now present Exhibit "B"—another example of the Depravation Play.

The West Player was leading in a rather close game; the North player was an Expert; the other players were also seasoned.

NORTH
♠ 9 7
♡ J 8 4 2
◇ A K Q 7 6
♣ 7 2

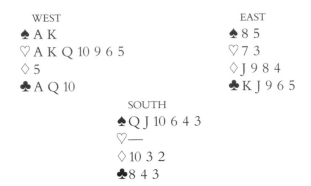

```
              WEST                              EAST
          ♠ A K                            ♠ 8 5
          ♡ A K Q 10 9 6 5                 ♡ 7 3
          ◇ 5                              ◇ J 9 8 4
          ♣ A Q 10                         ♣ K J 9 6 5
                          SOUTH
                      ♠ Q J 10 6 4 3
                      ♡ —
                      ◇ 10 3 2
                      ♣ 8 4 3
```

It was another "keeper" hand, and West could not believe his eyes! If he could slide the singleton diamond by his opponents, and if the King of clubs appeared early, this "puppy" might reach the Moon! Afterall, the hearts were pretty darn solid. South loved his hand, too. There were lots of spades for his Queen, and nice low cards in the minor suits. We had two rather happy campers!

North led the deuce of clubs, and when East played the King, West strained to conceal his joy, as he ducked with the tenspot. East now played his spade eight, South followed with the Jack, and the King held the trick. Now West held his breath as he eased his singleton diamond on the table, hoping for no heart discard. North grabbed the Ace and returned another spade. Note: Middle card discards are irrelevant.

West muttered, "God, am I good," as he took the Ace, and cashed his two high clubs. He then said, "Hold on everyone, it's going to be a bumpy ride!" Down came the Ace of hearts, as West said "Sometimes I impress myself!" South, with a truly great hand, decided to hold the Queen of spades for some unknown reason. After all, the spade Queen had no hope of stopping anything. West persisted with the King, and North knew that West had all the remaining hearts after this trick. He also wondered why the spade Queen had not appeared—especially since West was the low player and had nothing but hearts in his hand. Now came the heart Queen, and North thought that surely the spade Queen would appear on THIS trick! Therefore, he held his Jack of hearts. Now the heart ten was covered by the Jack. East complimented North on his fine defense. South released the spade Queen, and gurgled with total glee, as he said to North, "congratulations—it's a girl!"

I cannot quote the comments from North; after all, this is a "family book." The language was rough and the table shook!

As I said earlier, it is not nice to punish the player who stops the Moonshot. After all, that player is helping YOU as well. The "Depravation Play" may be worth a few laughs, but it will certainly leave a long lasting impression on the player who is the victim. Hearts is inherently a vicious game, but there are ethics and standards of play. Although South's antics may have been amusing, they were certainly irregular and cause for concern. Most players will not tolerate such behavior, and any offending person will not be invited for a second game. Winning is nice, but sportsmanship and congeniality are just as important. When the game is conducted at a high level, with solid technique, it can be truly fantastic.

Jack Soderlund was the finest player I ever met. He was a true gentleman at the Hearts table, and an absolute perfectionist. The next hand is a joy to behold—a rare example of the Variety II Squeeze, named after Jack. It is most appropriate that the prettiest play in Hearts is called the "Soderlund Squeeze."

# Chapter Nine
# FINAL HAND: THE GRAND SQUASH

   This beautiful hand was played in the final round of the 1978 National Open Tournament. The squash play in Hearts is very rare and I have only seen three examples during the past twenty years.

   This play is attributable to the peculiar qualities of the Queen of spades. Although she is a member of the spade suit, her thirteen-point value gives her a heartlike identity. Once in a great while, we see this dual personality manifested in a true squeeze capacity—with some subtle variations from the bridge maneuver.

   Jack Soderlund, of Tewksbury, Massachusetts, the first Hearts Life Master, executed this brilliant play. He also earned himself a special niche in the "Hall of Fame."

   Soderlund (West) was surprised to find that no low heart had been passed to him by the experienced South, who had good reason to keep his dry deuce.

   Soderlund kept his ♠A, hoping to catch the ♠Q and then run his solid hearts for slam.

   The ♣2 went to the King, for West ducked. Afraid to open a spade, East led his safe ◇5, ducked to North's Jack. The ♠7 shift went to South's eightspot, which all ducked. South cleared his clubs with the four, going to West's Ace. West led his ◇Q; South ducked. Fearing a heart pitch on the ◊K, West cashed his ♠A. North shed a high heart, but South defended brilliantly and held back his ♠Q. West surmised that the ◊A was in South's hand, and probably the ♠Q also. If so, the rest would be easy.

DEAL 25
*The Grand Squash*

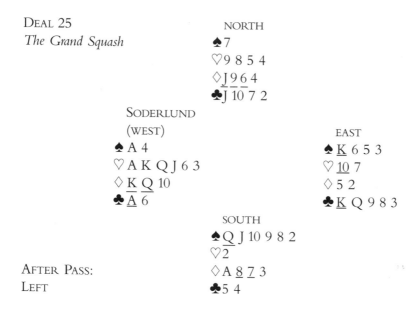

NORTH
♠ 7
♡ 9 8 5 4
◊ J 9 6 4
♣ J 10 7 2

SODERLUND
(WEST)
♠ A 4
♡ A K Q J 6 3
◊ K Q 10
♣ A 6

EAST
♠ K 6 5 3
♡ 10 7
◊ 5 2
♣ K Q 9 8 3

SOUTH
♠ Q J 10 9 8 2
♡ 2
◊ A 8 7 3
♣ 5 4

AFTER PASS:
LEFT

So West ran his five top hearts, leaving:

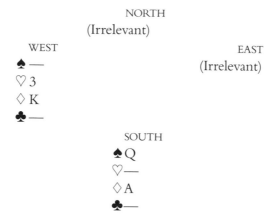

NORTH
(Irrelevant)

WEST
♠ —
♡ 3
◊ K
♣ —

EAST
(Irrelevant)

SOUTH
♠ Q
♡ —
◊ A
♣ —

When West led his ♡3 he utterly squashed South. South's saving discard was as easy to find as a million dollars lying in the gutter.

The spade discard would have been an instant surrender, so South shed his ◇A, hoping that West did *not* hold the now established King.

South rose to offer congratulations, and the kibitzers applauded. This is an example of the only pure squash play in Hearts. Its execution is part of the thrill of the game.

This play differs utterly from the squeeze play in bridge, for there you must have a partner who holds a quick entry down to the very end.

# Chapter Ten
# "A DAY IN THE LIFE"
# (DIARY OF A HEARTS PLAYER)

Once in a great while, perhaps every few years, a very special game occurs. I am sure we all can recall our best efforts in Chess, Rummy, Backgammon, Bridge, Scrabble, Cribbage, etc. I have played or observed several thousand Hearts games and vividly recall the incredible play of gifted individuals. I have seen many "escapes" from hopeless situations. There are several great hands in this book—which illustrate truly wonderful technique. (Refer to: "Soderlund Squeeze," "Vienna Coup," and "The Endplay.") The game narrated below is a true classic, and is representative of Hearts at its best (and sometimes worst)!!

Partnership play is the epitome of the team concept in many card games—and Hearts is no exception. In early June of 1998, I had the pleasure of participating in a Challenge Match with three of the best players in the Zone. I expected to have a good time and stimulating competition. What ensued was the most intense, frustrating, and emotional game I have ever played. And the ending is absolutely spectacular! Let's set the stage: Please note that the names of our opponents have been changed in order in order to protect their identity. (Smile!)

My partner was Eccy; the opponents will remain unnamed. Let me state quite clearly that they were (and still are) one of the premier partnership pairs in the Zone! Remember, we were playing the "Variety

II" game—in which there were four individual scores and the partners (who sat opposite each other) combined their scores together. The game ended when any player scored 100 (or more) points, and a team could not "Shoot the Moon" together—only individually.

### Hand #1—Eccy 12; Joe 0; Ms. "X" 14; Mr. "Y" 0 (We 12; They 14)

NOTE—INDIVIDUAL SCORES AFTER EACH HAND ARE LISTED AND THEN A SUMMARY FOR EACH TEAM ("WE/THEY"). We got off to a decent start as we planted the spade Queen on Ms. "X," but absorbed a raft of hearts on some weak side suits. This was to be our first and only lead until very late in the game.

### Hand #2—Eccy 32; Joe 6; Ms. "X" 14; Mr. "Y" 0 (We 38; They 14)

This was the first of three CONSECUTIVE hands in which Mr. "Y" was void in clubs after the pass. Ms. "X" promptly grabbed the lead with the Ace of clubs, and immediately led the three. Twice my poor partner had to play a middle club and Mr. "Y" let the spade Queen fly! It's too bad it was not the Standard Partners Game—we took twenty-six points together! Thus, they grabbed the lead and proceeded to destroy us!

### Hand #3—Eccy 53; Joe 7; Ms. "X" 18; Mr. "Y" 0 (We 60; They 18)

Yes sir—another three of clubs lead by Ms. "X" on trick two; another spade Queen on my partner, and a nice comfortable four points for them! It is so wonderful when you have the control card in a suit, and your partner holds the spade Queen.

### Hand #4—Eccy 61; Joe 21; Ms. "X" 18; Mr. "Y" 4 (We 82; They 22)

This was a "keeper" hand, and I expected a "normal" distribution of suits. I held the K J 4 of clubs. My partner led the deuce, Mr. "Y" showed out (absolutely amazing for a "hold" hand!), I tried the King, and Ms. "X" played the Ace. When her three of clubs hit the table, I printed in large capital letters "AGAIN??!!," as my partner played the eight, Mr. "Y" dumped another spade Queen, and I chose to overtake with the Jack to prevent my partner from reaching the 70 point barrier.

### Hand #5—Eccy 79; Joe 21; Ms. "X" 26; Mr. "Y" 4 (We 100; They 30)

If the last three hands did not dampen our enthusiasm, this one did. I was petrified when Mr. "Y" took the opening lead with King of clubs, and shifted to a middle diamond. I had seven spades, and the Ace of diamonds. Up I went—and I played the spade ten. Ms. "Y" took this with the Jack, and played the King of diamonds. My partner played the nine, and Mr. "Y" played the three. Now Ms. "X" tried the diamond two, Eccy had to follow with the six, another spade Queen flew out of Mr. "Y" 's hand, and yours truly played the four.

Four Queens in a row—all on control cards. We had no defense. For all intents and purposes, we could have set our play for "auto", or let a "Bot" (computer player) take over. It would have made no difference.

### Hand #6—Eccy 81; Joe 40; Ms. "X" 26; Mr. "Y" 9 (We 121; They 35)

The result was very straightforward. After the pass, I held a balanced hand with 4-3-3-3 shape. Although I held the Queen and three other spades, the "backers" were very weak. Ms. "X" also held four spades—headed by the Jack. My partner held the A K 4 of spades. Mr. "Y" grabbed the opening lead and played a small spade. Eccy took the King and tried a middle diamond. Mr. "Y" came in with the King, and played his remaining spade. My partner now inserted her Ace, and exited with another middle diamond. Ms. "X" overtook my Jack with the diamond Queen, and promptly played the spade Jack and pushed the suit one more time—and down came my Queen. At least, that was a bit more normal. But the rout was on, as they extended their lead to almost 100 points!

### Hand #7—Eccy 81; Joe 53; Ms. "X" 26; Mr. "Y" 22 (We 134: They 48)

Finally, a break! We had a successful across pass, and I was able to drop Mr. "Y" 's weakly protected spade Queen in four rounds. Ms. "X" chose to discard high diamonds on my four spade leads. But Mr. "Y" had the low clubs, and was able to escape for just thirteen points, as I was trapped with a fistful of clubs and some now-established middle diamonds. Still, it felt good breaking the string of five consecutive Queens! They were happy, too—as they could now exchange points evenly with us and drive on to victory!

### Hand #8—Eccy 85; Joe 67; Ms. "X" 34; Mr. "Y" 22 (We 152; They 56)

By this time, kibitzers were flocking to the table! One observer said, "Oh my God," and another sent me an ICQ—asking if there was a world record for the most lopsided game ever played! Ms. "X" was gurgling with total glee. Mr. "Y," who was usually as quiet as a church mouse, commented on how unbelievable the score had become. To make a long story short, this was a "keeper" or hold hand, and yours truly was dealt a singleton Queen of spades, three low hearts, and a string of high diamonds. Sure enough, the Queen was driven out promptly, and when the dust settled, I bagged another fourteen points! Ms. "X" snagged two hearts tricks, but the eight points were barely a concern to her. I thought of the Triple Crown of Horse Racing Series, and how Secretariat had won the Belmont Stakes by thirty-one lengths. It reminded me so much of how large their lead had become.

### Hand #9—Eccy 88; Joe 82; Ms. "X" 42; Mr. "Y" 22) (We 170; They 64)

It was another miserable hand. Ms. "X"'s two of hearts nailed me in the end for another spade Queen from her partner, and they were delighted to take eight points. The situation was truly hopeless. We were both in dire straights. If either of us shot a Moon, it would also end the game. They had us by 106 points!! I thought of resigning, but that would only add to the humiliation. I recalled the Battle of the Bulge (December, 1944) in which the Germans had the Americans surrounded at Bastogne. When the American commander (I believe his name was General MacAuliffe) was asked to surrender, his reply was one word—"Nuts"! Thus, I knew we would never quit, but it sure looked bleak!

### Hand #10—Eccy 88; Joe 83; Ms. "X" 42; Mr. "Y" 47 (We 171; They 89)

Mr. "Y" was dealt an absolutely atrocious hand, and an early heart discard on a diamond trick was taken by us. Eccy and I were able to duck everything in sight after that, and Mr. "Y" woofed twenty-five crispy

points. At this point, I was pleased that we were losing by double figures only! We were hoping for a respectable final score at this point.

### Hand #11—Eccy 88; Joe 83; Ms. "X" 50; Mr. "Y" 65 (We 171; They 115)

This was the across pass, and they had done so well with these hands.
However, disaster struck as communications broke down while they
were trying for a game-ending Moon. Mr. "Y" was running spades
and then clubs, but Ms. "X" forgot to unblock her Jack of clubs, and
she was forced into the lead. I was very happy to paint this trick with
a heart and break their Moon, separating the points. And, we escaped
with a nice clean zero!

### Hand #12—Eccy 92; Joe 83; Ms. "X" 70; Mr. "Y" 67 (We 175; They 137)

Another keeper hand was upon us, and I breathed a sigh of relief as I
looked at my cards. All I could do was hope that Eccy had a decent
hand as well. Ms. "X" had a badly placed Ace of spades, and took the
Queen on the third round of the suit. We had to take the King of
hearts to stop a possible Moon, but still came out with only four
points. Finally, the score was respectable! Now, I saw a faint glimmer
of hope . . .

### Hand #13—Eccy 92; Joe 83; Ms. "X" 82; Mr. "Y" 81 (We 175; They 163)

Now our spirits were really soaring! Once again, our opponents had a
complete misunderstanding during another Moon attempt, and once
again, they split twenty-six points between them. The post-mortems
were sure flying back and forth! They were on each other's cases!
Hearts is game replete with hindsight and second-guessing, and it had
become a factor. At this point, I knew the game was "up for grabs."
Our comeback was almost complete—and I felt the ever-growing
army of kibitzers was on our side. I could smell victory! I must hon-
estly admit that I was preparing a victory speech about how we had
staged the "greatest comeback of all time."

### Hand #14—Eccy 92; Joe 86; Ms. "X" 87; Mr. "Y" 99 (We 178; They 186)

This was a wonderful hand, and was hard fought to the end. We grabbed the first heart discard, and then my partner was on lead. I had a super hand with a well-protected spade Queen. Eccy proceeded to push three rounds of middle diamonds, and when Mr. "Y" finally had to go high—I was elated! I unloaded the Queen with great glee and fanfare. Then he led the Ace of hearts, and I said to myself—Wow! He is going out! Incredible! But he did not go out. He stopped at ninety-nine, after woofing eighteen points. A strategic heart deuce saved him for another day. Ninety-nine points. So close! After thirteen hands, we finally took the lead by eight points, but the ever dangerous across-pass was coming. I had a bad feeling about this! I really believed that the Hearts gods were on our side, and we did not deserve to lose. Still, a gnawing doubt was there. . . .

### Hand #15—Eccy 118; Joe 112; Ms. "X" 113; Mr. "Y" 99 (We 230; They 212)

And so, the "Final Roundup" came to pass. After the across exchange of cards, I did feel rather nice about my hand. The hand started out innocently. I had a string of top clubs, and four diamonds, K Q J 5, and two spades, and ten and four. (I was void in hearts). "If only two spades went through, and the diamond Ace appeared—maybe, maybe, maybe." While visions of sugar plums danced in my head, Mr. "Y" was preparing to launch a Moon rocket! I took the first club, as my suit was set up, and led the spade four. Mr. "Y" pounced on this, and immediately led the eight of diamonds—his only losing card. I inserted the King, and paused for thought. If I tried to cash a string of clubs in order to draw a heart, surely either opponent would hit me with the spade Queen. Then, at the end I would lose a diamond to the Ace or my spade ten to a spade honor, and the Moon would be stopped. Since my minor suit cards were very high, either a club or diamond lead would throw me back in for a raft of points. Certainly, this was a lousy way to lose.

Thus, I chose to duck Mr. "Y" 's diamond lead. That was the last decision that my partner and I made. Mr. "Y" announced "TRAM" (the rest are mine), and proceeded to cash out his incredibly long spade suit (after the pass, he held ten spades, two diamonds, and one club). His last card was the Ace of diamonds, and when it hit the table, the game was over. What a way to lose! The only Moon of the entire match, and it was ice-cold. We had no defense.

We were totally drained, and after the compulsory congratulations, it was time to call it a night. I have never played a game of Hearts which had every possible emotion on display. Luck, skill, deception, and finesse were all featured in a most thrilling match!

And thus, I bid you all farewell—enjoy Hearts—it's a great game!

# YOU GOTTA HATE HEARTS

(Sung to the song "You Gotta Have Heart" by the Damn Yankees)

You gotta play Hearts,
where the points hit you like darts,
It's a horrible crime
You eat the Queen the first time,
And then it starts,
You start to hate Hearts.

You're annoyed,
Cause the pass screwed up your void,
And now the Queen you just got
On that pass shows that you're not
Just paranoid,
You're annoyed.

You try to shoot,
But the cards don't distribute,
So instead of stayin' alive
You go and eat twenty-five,
A puppy shoot
Stinking suit.

Once again you lose
Cause you got no stinking two's
The language getting obscene
Your three just ate the Queen,
What's the use,
You just lose.

Use your smarts
Before your score goes off the charts,
The other players are low
You think you're safe but then NO!
Ouch! That smarts,
You gotta hate Hearts.

by Bruce Freedman
Woburn, MA

# Appendix One
# "UNCLE" JOE'S TEN WINNING HEARTS TIPS

## THE PASS

**1.** Do not keep the Queen of spades unless you have at least four low or three high spades accompanying her.

**2.** The Ace or King of spades is best passed when you have fewer than three other (supporting) spades in your hand.

**3.** Never pass a spade lower than the Queen.

**4.** You should pass to improve your hand, and not necessarily to "burn" your opponent.

## THE PLAY

**5.** If you hold the Queen of spades after the pass, try to "dump" her as soon as you can—unless your hand is *absolutely* safe.

**6.** Do not play for slam unless your hand contains the right combination of key cards. Don't even try for a Shoot with a losing heart!

**7.** It usually does not pay to take more than eight points to stop a slam. However, it may become necessary to take more points in order to avoid ending a game and finishing second or worse.

**8.** If you pass a low heart to an opponent (a good slam defense), and he leads *this card* after he has been burned with the Queen of spades, you should try to win *this trick*.

**9.** If a player does not lead spades early in the hand, you may assume he has spade problems (a weakly guarded Ace, King, or Queen).

**10.** Count those suits that are important to your hand, and be leery of unusually low discards by a particular player. A good strategy is to discard a heart early, which can disrupt the timing of a Slam attempt.

# Appendix Two
# GLOSSARY OF TERMS

Every game has its own terms, and Hearts is no exception. Yet many terms in Hearts, such as "Ace third," "balance," "consolation event," "discard," etc., are standard and traditional, coming straight from bridge and whist.

*We have tried to make this glossary as complete as possible,* and we have even included local colloquialisms that one day may become standard idiom. We hope that this glossary will serve you as a good quick-reference guide.

ACE THIRD: Classic bridge and whist idiom, literally meaning "Ace as the third card of its suit in hand," such as ◇A 5 2. Ace fourth is A x x x, nine fourth is 9 x x x, King fifth is K x x x x, Queen sixth is Q x x x x x, etc. (Honor cards should be mentioned collectively, e.g., A Q x x is called Ace-Queen fourth.)

ADVISORY BOARD: A group of elected experienced players who make policy and appoint and direct a card committee for each tournament, some of which may be staffed by the board's own members.

ANDREWS GAME: A seeded elimination tourney (i.e., one in which the stronger players are distributed among the tables ) where game is usually 125 points.

BACKER: A low or high-card guard to the ♠Q or other key card.

BALANCE: Remainder of tricks and/or scoring points.

**BLACK POINTS:** Basic heart points that count against a player.

**BOTTOM CARD:** Lowest-ranking card outstanding in its suit.

**BREAK:** (1) To discard or to lead a suit for the first time during a deal. (2) A(n) (un)lucky happenstance. A break may be good or bad.

**CALLOUS PALLAS:** The ♠Q, referred to in her usual black-widow-spider role.

**CARD COMMITTEE:** A group of volunteer better players organized to issue special local rules and to sit in court with players involved in a protested ruling.

**CASH:** To play a card so as to retain the lead.

**CHECK TOTAL:** For each deal twenty-six black points, rarely white instead. No player should settle for more or fewer points without director's approval.

**COLLINS GAMBIT:** Lead of the Queen from ♠Q x x on the third round of spades, with the hope of crashing or spearing the then-dry Ace or King.

**COMPARISON HEARTS:** More descriptive term for duplicate Hearts because this game's purpose is to allow comparison of scores earned on identical hands.

**CONSOLATION EVENT:** A special game held for players eliminated from a championship event and usually open to any other players as a side game.

**CONTROL CARD:** Usually the lowest-ranking card of a suit; sometimes the highest. Applies either at the beginning of play or later, after lower or higher cards have been played.

**COVER:** To follow suit higher than the last card played to the trick.

**CRASH:** To force an Honor (q.v.) card into play by playing another of the same suit. The Spear (q.v.) play is a form of crash play.

**DEFENSIVE HEARTS:** Style of play in which one makes a safe pass and plays that are aimed at stopping possible enemy slams.

**DEPRAVATION PLAY:** An unethical or vicious play without any logic or reason, e.g., holding the spade Queen as "punishment" for the player who stops a Slam.

**DIRECTOR:** Official referee and terminal scorer of a section or two.

**DISCARD:** The play of any card when unable to follow suit.

**DOUBLE SPEAR:** A lead of the ♠Q that forces two opponents to play the Ace and the King on the same trick.

**DOUBLES:** Partnership hearts; a game in which every player has one partner; pairs.

**DOUBLETON:** Two cards only, of a given suit, in a player's hand.

**DROP:** To play a card when you are not on lead (usually to rid yourself of an unwanted card); to force a card into play; to be forced into play (said of the card itself). A dropped card may either follow suit or be a discard.

**DRY:** Said of a card that is a singleton.

**DUCK:** To follow suit lower than the best or expected best card on the trick.

**DUPLICATE HEARTS:** See Comparison Hearts.

**EAT:** To be forced to capture (undesirable cards).

**ELIMINATION:** (1) Like KO (q.v.) but with less than half the field washed out after each round, group of rounds, or session. (2) Preparation for an endplay.

**ENDPLAY:** Stripping an opponent, then throwing him on lead to force a desired return.

**EXIT:** To lead a low card so as to give up the lead, usually for the rest of the hand.

**FANMAN MANEUVER:** The deceptive lead of a spade from Q x or Q x x. The idea is to convince the opponents that YOU do not hold the spade Queen.

**FINESSE:** The attempt to gain power for your lower-ranking cards by taking advantage of the position of higher-ranking cards held by opponents. (For example, you hold $\diamond$A Q. If your RHO holds the $\diamond$K, you can probably win two tricks if you play the $\diamond$Q when any other player leads a low card of the same suit.)

**FIX:** A bad result beyond your control. (Term from bridge.)

**FOLLOW SUIT:** To play a card of the same suit as the card led.

**FREEDMAN QUEEN:** Escaping from a bad hand with only thirteen points and no hearts.

**FREE ENTRY:** Entrance to a game without paying a fee; a free game.

**FREE JACK:** In the game where the $\diamond$J scores ten white points, if the $\diamond$J is led up to so that it wins positionally, it is called a free Jack.

**FREE PLAY:** Free ticket to a future game; often awarded as a prize.

**FRESH DEAL:** A new shuffle, cut, and deal for every hand played at every table; the term implies a procedure the opposite of that followed in Comparison (or Duplicate) Hearts (q.v.).

**GO FOR OR GOFOR:** To go for a slam; a hand with good slam chances; a player trying for slam.

**GOPHER:** Alternate spelling of Go For (q.v.).

**GRAND SLAM:** In the ◊J game, the capture of all fifteen scoring cards by one player, who scores thirty-six white points for this feat.

**GRAY GAMBIT:** Deliberate sacrifice that is ethically dubious.

**HARRIET'S "PHONY" MOON:** Holding a hopeless hand with a singleton or doubleton spade Queen, lots of high cards in the minor suits, and a losing heart. Several high cards are cashed, and then the Queen of spades is led. The hope is that an opponent will grab the Queen, thinking he/she is stopping a Moon. Variation—Applying same strategy with singleton Ace or King of spades.

**HEARTS-100:** Hearts where game ends when someone has scored 100 black points. Similarly with Hearts-125, etc.

**HEARTS POINTS:** One point (normally a black point) for each heart captured.

**HECTOR:** Official name for the ◊J since 1812.

**HIGH:** High-ranking; said of a card.

**HOG:** Player who intentionally avoids winning a few black points, even though he would stop a slam by doing so; or one who rarely passes a low heart as defense against slam.

**HONOR:** A high card, Ace through ten.

**HOSTESS OR HOST:** At a Hearts tourney, usually a volunteer greeter to direct arriving players to the registration desk and/or to other tourney-involved activities.

**HOUSE PLAYER:** Director-appointed person to fill in and complete a table that is short one or two players.

**INDIVIDUALS:** As in bridge, a partnership game where players change partners after each round, yet each player scores alone for himself.

**JACK OF DIAMONDS:** Card sometimes used to score ten white points for its captor; the game where this occurs.

**KO GAME:** Tourney where the two highest-scoring players at every table are KO'd (knocked out of the section) on every round. The KO'd players usually transfer at once into a consolation or second-chance section.

**LADY LAUREN CONVENTION:** Partnership Hearts passing system for across exchange with partner. One player agrees to pass hearts only and the other agrees to pass spades only to each other. It works well with Variation II Partners' format.

**LATE PLAY:** Play that is suspended at a table until the session ends.

**LEAD:** To play the first card of a trick; the play of this card. In Hearts, bridge, and whist every lead goes *from* the leader, *through* second hand, *toward* third hand, and *up to* fourth hand.

**LHO:** Left hand opponent, that player on your immediate left.

**LITTLE SLAM:** Used in connection with a "poop shoot," one player's taking twenty-five black points in one deal; it has been proposed (in a radical new idea) that he score thirteen *white* points and that the opponent who scored one black point also be grated thirteen white points instead as a special award for stopping a regular full slam of twenty-six points—this is a "little slam."

**LOL:** Little Old Lady; left on lead, implying that the player has no way to avoid taking all the rest of the tricks.

**LOW:** Low-ranking; said of a card. Such a card is sometimes incorrectly called little or small.

**MASTER CARD:** The highest-ranking card of a suit remaining at the table at a given stage of play.

**MASTER POINT:** Award for winning or placing high in one section or more when playing one session or more. Usually major awards stem from a national body.

**MATCH POINTS:** Points scored in party or tourney play, consisting of one point for each player beaten.

**MEET:** Meeting of two players as table opponents for one round; sometimes called a match.

**MIDDLE:** Midrank (q.v.).

**MIDRANK:** An intermediate card, often poison to a player holding several such cards; usually a Jack through a six, rarely higher or lower.

**MOONSHOT:** An attempt to score slam; a slam. (Informal term.)

**OAT:** Opponent across the table.

**OVERLOADED QUEEN:** Five or six-card spade suit that includes the Queen and is vulnerable in endplay against an opponent also long in spades.

**PALLAS:** Since 1812, the official name for the Queen of spades (unofficially called the black widow, etc.).

**PARLOR HEARTS:** A one-table game, with three or more players, in one's home, on a boat, plane, or train, etc.; any strictly informal game for fun only.

**PARTNERSHIP HEARTS:** Doubles (q.v.).

**PARTNERSHIP HEARTS, STANDARD GAME:** A game in which each player has a partner and scores are combined ("WE/THEY"). The team can Shoot the Moon together or separately. Game ends when either team scores 100.

**PARTNERSHIP HEARTS, VARIETY II:** A "hybrid" pairs or team game where players still have a partner; however, the scores are maintained individually. A successful Slam is made by one of the partners, who must take all of the points by him/herself. Game ends when either partner reaches 100 points. Low combined score wins.

**PARTY HEARTS (OR PARTY):** Two or more tables in a formal movement in which the playing is only for fun and/or for frivolous prizes.

**PAT:** Pass across the table.

**PER-PLAYER POINTS:** The number of black points, assessed for committing an irregularity, that the director subtracts from every nonoffender's score and adds in toto to the offender's score.

**PIONEER:** A player new to party and/or tourney hearts; a novice.

**PITCH:** To discard.

**PLAY PERIOD:** The time elapsed from the laying face down of the first pass card (or opening lead if no pass is made) at a table through the final agreement on scores and the entry of the scores of a deal.

**POOP SHOOT:** Colloquial for an unfortunate player's scoring twenty-five black points in one deal; this, however, is not unfortunate if playing Little Slam (q.v.).

**PROTEST PERIOD:** That time allowed by the director—usually thirty to sixty minutes after a session ends—in which a player may protest in writing a director's ruling or an alleged error in a terminal score. On expiration of protest period all scores become final and cannot be changed regardless of error.

**PTL:** Pass to left.

**PTR:** Pass to right.

**QUARTET:** One table of any four-handed game of hearts.

**QUEEN THIRD:** Queen and two lower cards; Queen fourth is Queen and three lower cards, etc. See also Ace Third.

**RABBIT:** A weak player or a novice; synonymous with palooka, duffer, turkey, etc.

**RENOUNCE:** To discard when able to follow suit; informally, to renege.

**REPEAT MEET:** Play against the same player for a second round.

**REVENGE MEET:** Opposing the same player on one round more than the field.

**RHO:** Right hand opponent, that player on your immediate right.

**ROSNER SPLIT:** Extraordinary distribution of the heart suit, resulting in the stopping of slams. (For example, a player holding ♡A K Q 10 x x x x discovers that another player holds ♡J x x x.)

**ROSNER SUICIDE PASS:** To pass the ♠A x, ♠K x, or ♠Q x to an opponent, hoping not to receive the dry ♠Q.

**ROTATIONS, PASSING:** Left, right, across (then repeat). Variations— "Scatter" pass (see definition); "Keeper" or hold hand—no pass is made at all. This option occurs on the fourth deal of each hand.

**ROUND:** A prearranged number of deals, often four, or six to twenty in Hearts-125, after which players total their scores, then go to other tables.

**ROVER:** Extra player who displaces a different player on every deal and/or round.

**RUBIN MANEUVER:** Pass of the ♠Q from good spade length, followed by persistent spade leads to smoke out the Queen.

**RUN:** To lead a suit repeatedly in the hope of smoking out a card or cards.

**SANDBAGGER:** A strong player pretending to be weak in order to fool strangers; a player who lies in wait to trap an unsuspecting victim.

**SCATTER (OR SCRAMBLE) PASS:** Pass of one card to one opponent and two cards to another, or one card to each of all (usually three) opponents.

**SESSION:** Usually play for one afternoon or evening, rarely a longer time when a special movement requires about four hours or more to complete.

**SHAPE:** The relative distribution of the four suits in a player's hand. (For example, a hand with a 1-6-4-2 shape has one spade, six hearts, four diamonds, and two clubs.)

**SHILL:** One who procures players ("lobsters") for a dishonest money game.

**SHOOT THE MOON:** To try to make a slam.

**SINGLES:** The common form of Hearts, with no partnership.

**SINGLETON:** Solitary card of its suit in a player's hand.

**SLAM:** The capture of all thirteen hearts and the ♠Q by one player, scoring twenty-six white points; to make such a capture.

**SMALL SLAM:** In the Jack of Diamonds variant, the capture of the ♠Q and thirteen hearts, but not the ◊J, by one player. Compare with Grand Slam (q.v.).

**SMOKE:** To attempt persistently to force an opponent's card (frequently the ♠Q) or cards into play.

**SMUDGE:** In John Draper Woodfin's group of players, a synonym for "slam."

**SPEAR:** To lead the ♠Q in order to crash the dry Ace or King, maybe both.

**SPLIT:** Lie of a suit in the hands of your three opponents, or two opponents if the third is known to be out of the suit in question.

**SPOT:** A card ranking ten or lower; the Ace; any nonpicture card.

**STANZA:** One or two or more special groups of rounds within a session; a subsession, so to speak, but never called this.

**STILL PACK:** A second pack of cards, to be shuffled by a dealer's OAT for dealer's LHO, the next dealer.

**STREWN:** Said of players changed irregularly, in a scattered fashion.

**STRIP:** To lead a suit so as to draw entry or exit cards from a hand.

**SUBTRACTER:** White points; they are subtracted from one's score.

**SWAP:** A pass in which two players exchange cards, as in the common pass across the table.

**SWISS HEARTS:** A progressive party where winners move up one table.

**SYNCOPATION:** In a round, the rotation of players around the usually stationary North player after each deal or two; a movement within the movement of rounds. This is common in individual tourneys in bridge, in order to change partners more often.

**THIRTEENER:** Last unplayed card of a suit.

**TOP CARD:** The highest-ranking card outstanding in its suit.

**TOTAL POINTS:** The simple addition of each player's black points to determine the winner of a game (the player with the fewest). Distinguished from Match Points (q.v.).

**TOURNAMENT:** A superior tourney, usually played for a regional, national, or world title.

**TOURNEY:** Two or more tables of serious play for master points, substantial prizes, and/or an annual club, city, county, or state title; a minor tournament.

**TRIPLE DUMMY:** A special form of three-handed hearts in which two jokers are used as extra bottom-rank clubs and there are six nine-card hands. As in bridge, each player holds two hands, his own closed hand and his exposed dummy opposite him.

**TRIPLE SPEAR:** A Double Spear play (q.v.) that forces a heart discard on the same trick.

**TRISECT PASS:** The pass of one card to each of (usually) all three opponents.

**TURKEY:** A novice or weak player, also familiarly and jocularly called a duffer, bumble-puppy, rabbit, etc.

**UP:** The direction of the next higher-numbered table, usually southerly.

**VOLUNTEER:** A person who offers to fill in, if needed to complete that last table.

**WHITE POINTS:** Good points, subtracted from a player's score of black points; usually earned by making a slam.

# Appendix Three
# THE LAWS OF HEARTS

Until now, the game of Hearts had no proper set of laws, and there were insufficient penalties for some irregularities and none for others. Here are the twenty-six Official General Laws of Hearts for the standard quartet singles game in parties and tourneys, and for the closely related variants for three to seven players.

*(1) The Pack.* The game of Hearts is played with a standard pack of fifty-two cards, all of the same size, back design, and color, and consisting of thirteen cards in each of four suits. The suits are spades (♠), hearts (♡), diamonds (◇), and clubs (♣). The cards in each suit rank downward in the following order: Ace highest, then King, Queen, Jack, 10, 9, 8, 7, 6, 5, 4, 3, and 2 lowest. Rarely, jokers are added as special cards. It is incorrect to refer to any card as big or little or small, for all cards are of the same size. The *rank* of cards is called high or low, and intermediate-ranking cards—usually Jacks down through sixes—are called intermediate or midrank or middle.

*(2) The Number of Players.* Three to seven may play, rarely two in "honeymoon" variants (with each player playing for himself, these games are all "singles"). The best game, standard for parties and tourneys, is four-handed, called "quartet." Quartet games are usually singles, but in special four-handed tourney events there may be two-player partnerships—called "doubles"—or four-player teams-of-

four. Also, Hearts may be either the regular variety, with a fresh deal for every hand played, or the variety, analogous to duplicate bridge, called comparison (or duplicate) Hearts.

*(a) No Partner in Singles.* In singles no player may have a partner and no player may deliberately lose in order to help a "partner" win. A director and/or a rules committee may assess penalties and/or disciplinary action against any proven violation.

*(3) The Draw.* Any player shuffles the pack and spreads it out face-down upon the card table; then each player draws one card, which must not be one of the four cards at either end of the pack. If attention is brought to an irregular draw, the player involved must draw again; if two or more players draw irregularly, there must be a new shuffle, spread, and draw. That player drawing the *lowest* card deals first. Ties in rank are broken by following the order of suits in Law 1 above (spades high). An optional method is to let any player shuffle the pack and have it cut; then, beginning with his LHO, he deals one card at a time, face up. The first player to receive a heart or the ♠Q is the first dealer.

*(4) The Shuffle and Cut.* Any player may then shuffle, the dealer doing so last. The dealer then places the shuffled pack on his right, face down, to offer it to his RHO to cut. His RHO must cut the pack into two portions by lifting a packet of four to forty-seven cards and placing it to the left of the remaining portion. Then the dealer completes the cut by picking up this remaining portion and placing it atop the first portion. Meanwhile, where two packs are used, as is usually the case in tourney play, the player *opposite* the dealer (dealer's OAT) collects the still pack (the one not in use, usually from the previous deal), shuffles it, and places it on his *right* to mark his RHO as the next dealer.

The still pack must be identical with the one in use but must differ in the color or design on the backs of the cards (to enable one to distinguish between the packs if they are mixed up).

*(5) The Deal.* Cards must be served, one at a time, face down in clockwise rotation, beginning with dealer's LHO, to create four thirteen-card hands (in quartet games). For fewer or more than four players, deal cards as far as they will go and correct the indivisibility of the pack by one of the following adjustments: have each player who is dealt a surplus card play *two* cards to trick one; place surplus cards face down to

form a "widow" to go to the winner of trick one; use a slightly "stripped" deck; add jokers (when there are six or more players).

(a) At least three players at quartet must be present during the shuffle, cut, and deal, unless the director instructs otherwise.

(b) There must be a new shuffle, cut, and deal if, before the last card is served, any player points out that the deal is incorrect (e.g., the pack has not been cut) or that any player has seen the face of any card not his own, or if the director so deems for any good and sufficient reason.

(c) If before or during the play a card is found missing, the director must be summoned and he must institute a search for it. If found among played cards, Law 67 of the latest Laws of Duplicate Bridge shall be used as a guideline; if found elsewhere, it must be restored to the deficient hand of the player who is deemed to have held it originally, and in such case his failure to play it earlier may establish a revoke by him.

*(6) The Pass.* After looking at his cards just dealt to him, each player must pass three cards face down (four in trio Hearts, two in sextet and septet) to an opponent. By popular practice the first pass is to the left, the second across the table, and the third to the right; then on deal four the cycle is repeated. Alternatively, the cycle may first be lengthened with other types of passes. For example, North and East may swap while South and West copy, etc. In the crisscross pass, adjacent players pass across and the recipients pass right or left to their adjacent players—the original passers. In the split pass, two cards are passed to one opponent and one to another. And in the full scatter pass every player passes one card to every opponent.

There is another option, often called the "keeper" or "hold" hand. Here, there is no pass at all. A popular rotation is to have left, right, and across passes, followed by a no pass or "keeper" hand on every fourth deal. This option is at the discretion of each tournament director.

The advisory board (AB) or card committee (CC) may authorize or bar whatever passes seem, respectively, suitable or unsuitable, and may even prescribe no pass at all on specific deals. In doubles Hearts (partnership play) the pass to partner should be *optional,* at the discretion of the director or of the players themselves.

Every player must pass his three cards before looking at the face of any card passed to him. Penalty: any player at fault is assessed twenty-six black points, and the play of the deal is cancelled. The same penalty applies to a pass of too few or too many cards, and to a pass of cards to the wrong opponent if not corrected before any opponent sees the face of any card passed incorrectly to him.

*(7) The Object of the Game.* The object of the game is to *avoid* winning in tricks any heart cards and/or the ♠Q (called "point cards"), or, instead, to capture all fourteen of these cards. The latter capture is called a "slam," or, colloquially, a "moonshot" or "smudge."

*(8) The Opening Lead.* In order to lead or to play a card, the player detaches it from his hand and places it face up in front of himself on the table. Whoever holds the ♣2 must lead it on trick one. No player void of clubs may discard a point card on that trick, unless unavoidable. The penalty for violation is two black points per player (per-player black points or PBP) if any player subsequently plays to the trick, but the offender may correct his error without penalty if no one has played after him. In any case, if anyone calls next trick, any such error must be corrected, and any card played after it may be retracted without penalty.

None may lead a heart until a heart has been discarded or the ♠Q has been played. (For further details and stipulations, see the section, "Heart Lead Prohibited," in chapter 2).

*(9) The Play* The player on lead may play any card in his hand except as restricted by Law 8 above and by paragraph (c) below.

(a) After the lead each player in his clockwise turn plays a card, and the four cards (three in trio Hearts, etc.) so played constitute a trick. Each player must follow suit if possible; this takes precedence over all other requirements in these laws.

(b) The player who wins a trick leads to the next trick.

(c) *Discard.* If unable to follow suit, a player may play any card, called a "discard," except that he must not discard any point card on trick one or as otherwise restricted.

(d) *Played Card.* Each plays a card by detaching it from his hand and placing it face up upon the table. If such a card touches or nearly touches the table, or if it is held in such a position as to indicate clearly that it was played, it must be played; but the player may withdraw it to satisfy a penalty, if the play is illegal, or if a previous player to the trick changes his play legally.

(e) *Fifth Card.* A fifth card contributed to a trick in quartet Hearts may be withdrawn without penalty, unless the director deems it a lead to the next trick.

(f) **Lead out of Turn.** If a player leads out of turn, no penalty is levied against him if he retracts the card before anyone else has played, or even if someone has played after him and he had been misinformed that it was his turn to lead; otherwise, if the trick is incomplete, all who played after the wrong leader may retract their cards without penalty; a completed trick stands, and the offender is assessed a penalty of two per-player black points.

*(10) The Revoke.*

(a) **Renounce.** If a player discards when able to follow suit, he is said to "renounce," and there is no penalty if he corrects his renounce before any card is led to the next trick or if he renounces to trick twelve (or next-to-last trick). If discovered before the deal is scored, all trick-twelve and thirteen cards must be restored, then be played correctly without penalty.

After a renounce all players retract their played cards, and those who played before the renounce must again play the same cards that they did originally unless not retracted, but the renouncer corrects his play and a subsequent player may change his play.

If a revoke is established and all the point cards have been played before the revoke trick, there is no penalty, nor is there one if the revoke does not stop a slam.

(b) **Revoke.** If a proper lead has been made to the next trick, the undiscovered renounce becomes an established revoke, unless the renouncer has previously asked what suit was led and received no answer for ten seconds or longer, or if he was misinformed. The penalty for an established revoke is twenty-six black points against the offender, and all hands are thrown in without any further play.

THE FIVE-POINT RULE. If a predetermined number of points, not deals, constitute a game, and a revoke or other assessed penalty would raise the score of the offender above game or to within five points or fewer below game, he scores no game now. Instead, the penalty black points are added to his score; then game-level for him and him only becomes *five points more.* For example: if in Hearts-100 a revoke penalty Jacks up an offender's score to 97 or 110, five points more make his new game-level 102 or 115, respectively.

But if his score was four points or fewer below game *before* the revoke occurred, only this actual difference instead of five points is used to establish his new game-level. For example: if his score was 98 points before he revoked, he was only two points below game. If penalized 26 points to make 124, his new game-level is *two* points more, or 126.

(c) **Revoke Against a Slam Try.** If a revoke stops an otherwise un-stoppable slam, the slam scores and the offender is assessed four per-player black points. But if the slam can be defeated without the revoke, play ends and the revoking offender is assessed 26 black points.

(d) **Idle Revoke Carries No Penalty.** An idle revoke is one with no effect upon the score. A revoke on any trick with no scoring card there or left in any hand is harmless and idle and carries no penalty. If all point cards have been played (the ♠Q and the 13 hearts), then any revoke on the remaining "pointless tricks" carries no penalty. Players must keep their tricks *in order,* for any possible review. Also, a revoke made against a successful slam carries no penalty, unless the slam cannot be made without the revoke. But a player who revokes while making a slam loses his slam and suffers the revoke penalty of twenty-six black points.

**(11) Examining Quitted Tricks.** Any player may examine the last quitted trick provided that he has not led or played to the next trick. The penalty for a proven infraction is two per-player black points.

**(12) Exposure of Cards.** If a player exposes any of his own cards pre-maturely, he is not penalized (except in doubles Hearts); but if he ex-poses another player's cards, the penalty is two per-player black points (PBP) for the first such card and one PBP for each subsequent card, with a maximum of eight PBP in one deal. However, one card ex-posed out of turn may be ruled by the director as a lead out of turn if he deems that this was the player's intent.

If a player leads a heart illegally, the penalty is two PBP, yet there is no penalty if he corrects his error before anyone after him plays. (See also Law 22, below.)

**(13) Claims and Concessions.** If a player exposes his hand and claims all remaining tricks or point cards, he must announce the order of his plays. If he fails to announce, any other player may direct how he plays his cards. But no second player may join in this role, and no consulta-tion is allowed.

If a player concedes winning any thirteen or fewer point cards, he forfeits all rights to a better score. The director should try to adjust other players' scores so as to create the usual twenty-six point check total, but he may assess extra black or white points in the interests of equity by entering them in the excess-or-deficiency column (EOD) of the master or recapitulation score sheet.

*(14) Scoring.* Every heart that a player captures in a trick counts one black point, that is, one point against him, and the ♠Q counts thirteen black points; but if one player (or a partnership in doubles) captures all fourteen point cards, he scores twenty-six white points. In Hearts-100 he has the option of subtracting twenty-six from his own black-point score while all others score zero, or of adding twenty-six black points to each opponent's score while leaving his own score unchanged.

The winner of a game (the one with the lowest score) scores a bonus of eighteen white points (WP) and the runner-up eight WP per four deals of a round only on totals for the entire round, but nothing for a remainder of one to three deals in a round of five or more deals. Multiply these premiums by two in a game of eight to eleven deals, by three for one of twelve to fifteen deals, etc. In a three-deal round, premiums are eighteen and eight points as above, but in a two-deal round they are halved to nine and four.

(a) **Game.** In fresh-deal party or tourney play the game is 100 black points, but the director may alter this to satisfy time limits or for any other valid reason. In parties of more than fourteen tables, a round may be fixed at two to six deals to constitute a game, with all players then moving to face new opponents.

(b) **Match Points.** In fresh-deal play, as soon as one player at a table acquires enough points for game, play ends, and all scores are totalled and compared. The player scoring the fewest black points gets three match points (MP) for underscoring three opponents on the round, the player with the next fewest gets two MP, the player with the third fewest gets one, and the game player gets zero. Each MP represents one opponent beaten in a comparison of scores.

Ties each count one-half MP. But a slam scores six MP, with opponents each scoring zero. The AB or CC may alter these figures; they may wish to use victory points on a scale of, for example, 5-3-2-1, or instead, they may simply let players use total-point (cumulative black-point) scoring.

(c) **Application of Scoring.** Party and tourney Hearts are of four kinds: the long game, the short game, the barometer game, and deal-a-match, as follows:

(i) **The Long Game.** Also called Hearts-100, the long game is played rubber-bridge style in one long round of about eight to twenty deals, depending on how quickly a player scores game.

*(α) Curtailed Games.* If someone goes game at half or more of all the section's tables, the director may curtail play at all tables by letting each finish only its current deal (and then only if any card therein has already been dealt) and may then declare each lowest score as game winner at its table. Optionally, if all but one or two tables finish their game round simultaneously, the director may suspend play at the remaining table or two, and have the latter table or tables take a late play.

*(β) Score Intelligence.* Any player at any time, except during the play period of a deal, may see the score status of all his table mates and/or request and receive from table-captain North (if score keeper, otherwise from any player) the correct data. If he is misinformed and he can demonstrate damage to his interests before the play of the next deal begins, he may ask the director for an adjusted score. But inquiry during the play period renders the offender liable to a penalty of two per-player black points.

(ii) *The Short Game.* Each round finishes one short game, which is usually fixed at four deals, perhaps more or fewer to complete the movement within the time scheduled.

(iii) *The Barometer Game.* In this combination of long and short games, a long game is made to extend through several short rounds. It is called barometer Hearts because, as each round starts, the director posts all running scores at each table on a blackboard to help players adjust their strategies. As soon as anyone goes game in a section, the game ends throughout that section, but no one moves (unless the game is ended with a regular short round); instead, all start a new sectionwide game. The director awards match points for all the scores in that round in the section. If there are twenty players, the lowest cumulative scores fetches nineteen MP, the next-lowest eighteen MP, and so on.

The director may extend or curtail the last round of a completed movement by increasing or reducing the number of deals, in order to let some tables finish their own games, or to conform to tight time limits.

If players score in an unequal number of games, the match-point scores of players in the smaller number of games are factored up to par with those of players scoring in the largest number of games. A half match point or more as a fraction in a player's factored score is counted as one full point, less than one-half as zero. This breaks what might otherwise seem to be a tie.

(iv) **Deal-a-Match Hearts.** This name may apply to play for straight total points; in a better variant, the scores of every deal are converted into match points.

(d) **Scoring Limits.** No player may get more than twenty-six points in one deal.

(i) **Slam Scores.** Slam scoring has new practical variants. In one of these, if no player at a table can go game by adding twenty-six black points, then the slam winner must add twenty-six black points to the score of every opponent at this table. The purpose of this is to prevent a slam winner from instead of subtracting twenty-six black points from his own score and thus prolonging the game. Also, in a duplicate-Hearts variant, the only slam scores allowed are thirteen white points for the slam winner and thirteen black points against each opponent at his table.

**(15) Incorrect Movement.** If, any time after a player has looked at any card passed to him, anyone discovers that any player is at the wrong table and/or is playing the wrong board at duplicate Hearts,★ the current deal must be played out and scored. The director should be called at once. The offender is assessed two PBP, and any other player responsible for the gaffe at the same or another table is assessed one PBP. Of course, if the error is discovered before anyone looks at the face of a card passed to him, and the error is corrected, there is no penalty.

**(16) Irregularities.** Any active player may call attention to an irregularity; when this occurs, the director should be called at once. In this case any player may call him, although it is better for the table captain to do so. This action causes no player to lose rights to which he might be otherwise entitled. No player should resume play until the director has rectified all matters and assessed any penalties that may have been required. If the offender prematurely corrects his irregularity, he may suffer a further penalty.

**(17) Assessing Penalties.** Only the director has the right to assess or waive penalties. Players have no right to assess or waive on their own,

---

★Duplicate Hearts is in an experimental stage of development and is not recommended for standard-format play.

and the director may cancel any such action. Wherever these laws provide a choice of penalties, the director must explain all options.

*(18) Forfeit of Right to Penalize.* This right to penalize for an irregularity in play is forfeit if the nonoffending player whose turn it is to play acts before a legal penalty has been stated and imposed by the director. Alternately, the director may assess per-player points on such nonoffender.

If a spectator is the first to draw attention to an irregularity, the right to correct and/or penalize is forfeited if the offender or nonoffender, as the case may be, was responsible for the spectator's presence at the table; even so, the director may overrule this and assess a penalty at his discretion.

*(19) Discretionary Powers of Director.* The director may assign an adjusted score or scores if these laws fail to indemnify a nonoffender for a violation or an impropriety committed by an opponent. A director may assign no adjusted score on the basis that the penalty provided by these laws is either unduly severe or advantageous to other players.

*(20) Adjusting Scores.* A score is adjusted by adding black points to an offender's score and subtracting the total of penalty points, divided evenly, from other players' scores. Usually the number of black points subtracted from nonoffenders' scores in sum should equal points added to the offender's score, yet the director for a good and sufficient reason may assess extra points and have these entered in a special excess-or-deficiency column (EOD) on the master or recapitulation score sheet.

*(21) Play after an Illegal Play.* If a player plays after an illegal play by his RHO, such as an out-of-turn or premature lead, he must call the director's attention to the irregularity. If he fails to do so before another player plays after him, he may be assessed two PBP. If he is the fourth (or last) player to the trick and a legal lead is made to the next trick, the gaffe stands uncorrected and unpenalized.

*(22) Question of Procedure.* No player may ask if any point card has been discarded or played. Each player has a responsibility to keep track of all plays and discards of hearts and the ♠Q. But if a player leads a heart illegally and no lead has been made to the next trick, the lead and plays are corrected as above, and the offender is assessed two PBP.

*(23) Simultaneous Play.* If two players each play a card simultaneously to a trick, the second player is deemed to have played in his proper turn.

# Appendix Four
# DUPLICATE HEARTS (THE ANDREWS FORMAT)

The Duplicate concept has been used in the game of Bridge for more than fifty years. It is the ideal method of measuring the skill level of individuals or partners. The American Contract Bridge League (Memphis, TN) conducts thousands of these events every year at all levels, including National Championships.

Duplicate Hearts is a new concept, combining the best features of the standard (fresh-deal) game within a new format. In ordinary Hearts, as in Rubber Bridge, you compete against only the players at your table. Each hand is dealt at random, played once, scored, and is gone forever.

In Duplicate Hearts, each hand travels from one table to another, and is played under identical conditions at each table. At the conclusion of the event, your scores are then compared to those of each player who held the SAME cards as you did. This is the ideal game for those who wish to become accomplished players, as well as those who seek an accurate measure of their skill. The Duplicate Board serves two important functions. First, it makes it possible to pass the four hands of each deal from table to table in order to allow replay of the same hand by others. Second, it establishes the condition under which the board is played. The board has a number, compass direction, and pass direction for a particular hand.

In the typical tournament, each player is assigned a number, and goes to a designated table for the first round. Because Hearts is a "solo" game, an individual's movement is used for most events. (There is also a Partners' Duplicate format.) This version can be played with a pass as well, although, it is much easier to have all "hold" hands. (The comparison aspect changes with the pass.) A round consists of four hands, and then you move to a different table to meet new opponents and a fresh set of four new hands. All the rules of the game still apply. At the end of the session, your scores for all of the hands that you played are compared to the scores of those players who held the same hands. The boards are then match pointed, and the results are posted to a "recap" sheet. At the end of the session, the best scorer in each direction (N, S, E, and W) play in a regular finals.

This is a very easy version to master, and will be used for major tournament qualifying rounds. It is also easily adapted for Internet play, as the site computer can easily distribute and control each hand.

For more information on the variations of Hearts and other card games, please contact this site: (www.pagat.com/)

John McLeod of Great Britain is the world's leading authority on all card games, and has compiled some truly fascinating information. His site is an explorer's paradise!

# Appendix Five
# THE INTERNET AND HEARTS-RELATED SOFTWARE

The rise of the Internet and World Wide Web have expanded the horizons of Hearts players everywhere. Now, any player with access to a computer (and modem) can play a good game of Hearts with quality opponents. There are many sites featuring all sorts of card, board, and action games. Listed below are the best Internet locations for the game of Hearts. Included are reviews and acess information.

## 1. MICROSOFT INTERNET GAMING ZONE
## (www.zone.com)

This is the premier site on the Internet, featuring a wide variety of games. The graphics are superb, and most of the Hearts and Spades rooms are very accessible. Special and invitational competitions are conducted on a regular basis. All skill levels are represented. The cards are very easy to read, and each game flows smoothly. Rules and strategy are explained quite clearly. A monthly column is also published, and there are some great instructional articles. Several dedicated hosts help to maintain order and assist with tournament pairings. Also featured is a ratings system, and a wide variety of events. Two of the absolutely superb tournament locales with truly dedicated directors are:

Eclectic Hearts (www.eccy.com) and

Hot Dog Hearts (www.hotdoggames.com)

Try the Zone! You will like it!
There are also several other sites offering quality Hearts games. Here
are a few for your information.

## 2. M—PLAYER (www.mplayer.com)

This is one rather impressive location, with some of the fanciest de-
signs you will ever see! This is a multi-game site, with lots and lots of
tournaments and events. You will be very excited with the layout. The
plus program offers a wide array of additional services and features.
There is also a ratings system. It is certainly well worth your time to
check out this really outstanding and very "cool" site!

## 3. I-PLAY.NET (ONLINE MULTI-PLAYER GAMES SYSTEM) (www.Iplay.net)

I-PLAY certifies member players for competition in sanctioned card
tournaments on the Internet.

Membership is open to players over the age of eighteen who wish
to compete. Many events are held at the Iplay.net card realm.

This is a brand-new site, with a special approach to Hearts (and
other classic card games). A Universal Ratings System with an auto-
matic posting of completed games is one of the key features of I-PLAY.
A newsletter, seminars, and an annual convention are also offered.

## 4. OTHER HEARTS SITES: Here is a listing of other Internet locations for all levels of Hearts competitions:

a. Excite Home Games (www.excite.com/play)
    This is a nice, compact site with a lot of features, and it is con-
    stantly improving. One very clever innovation is the optional
    rules control.
b. Gamestorm Classic Card Games (www.gamestorm.com)
c. WorldPlay (www.worldplay.com)
    Please note that Gamestorm and World Play are offered as part of
    the America Online Internet Package.

## HEARTS-RELATED SOFTWARE AND INFORMATION

There are a number of very fine Hearts related CD-ROMs in the marketplace. These are ideal for the time when you cannot find "live" opponents, but still want a quality game. Here are a few very fine products with brief "review" comments:

1. Hearts Deluxe (Freeverse Software of New York City).

This is the best program for intermediate and advanced level of play. Gorgeous design, cute characters, and fine programming are the key features of this newly-updated product. It is a real challenge!

2. Bicycle Hearts/Spades (Expert Software of Coral Gables, FL)

Expert Software has produced this CD for a few years, as part of the US Playing Card Company's series. It is designed for novice and intermediate level of play. It is also an excellent teaching guide, and has very easy to read graphics.

## AMERICAN HEARTS AND SPADES PLAYERS' ASSN.

For more information on this national organization, refer to these Websites:

www.expertsoftware.com

www.freeverse.com/ahspa

AHSPA sponsors "live" Hearts and Spades tournaments, awards rating points, and sanctions a number of preferred Internet sites. There are twelve (U.S.) regions, as well as Canadian and international chapters. Contact "www.freeverse.com" for more information.